Lecture Notes in Bioinformatics 4780

Edited by S. Istrail, P. Pevzner, and M. Waterman

Subseries of Lecture Notes in Computer Science

Corrado Priami (Ed.)

Transactions on Computational Systems Biology VIII

 Springer

Series Editors

Sorin Istrail, Brown University, Providence, RI, USA
Pavel Pevzner, University of California, San Diego, CA, USA
Michael Waterman, University of Southern California, Los Angeles, CA, USA

Editor-in-Chief

Corrado Priami
The Microsoft Research - University of Trento
Centre for Computational and Systems Biology
Piazza Manci, 17, 38050 Povo (TN), Italy
E-mail: priami@dit.unitn.it

Library of Congress Control Number: 2007938331

CR Subject Classification (1998): J.3, F.1, F.4, I.6

LNCS Sublibrary: SL 8 – Bioinformatics

ISSN   1861-2075
ISBN-10   3-540-76638-3 Springer Berlin Heidelberg New York
ISBN-13   978-3-540-76638-4 Springer Berlin Heidelberg New York

Springer is a part of Springer Science+Business Media

springer.com

© Springer-Verlag Berlin Heidelberg 2007
Printed in Germany

Typesetting: Camera-ready by author, data conversion by Scientific Publishing Services, Chennai, India
Printed on acid-free paper   SPIN: 12187638   06/3180   5 4 3 2 1 0

Preface

This issue of the journal reports regular papers. The first contribution is by Falko Dressler and discusses self-organizing mechanisms in computer networks. The second contribution is by Preetam Ghosh, Samik Ghosh, Kalyan Basu and Sajal K. Das and deals with a stochastic event based simulation technique to estimate protein-ligand docking time. The third contribution is by Morteza Analoui and Shahram Jamali, and it deals with the interpretation of the Internet as a biological environment to study congestion phenomena. The fourth contribution is by Corrado Priami and it discusses how computational thinking in biology can be implemented through the use of process calculi. The last contribution is by Peter Saffrey, Ofer Margoninski, James Hetherington, Marta Varela-Rey, Sachie Yamaji, Anthony Finkelstein, David Bogle and Anne Warner and it deals with management information systems in biology. Finally we publish a corrected version of a paper by Ruet and Remy published in the previous volume of the journal.

July 2007   Corrado Priami

LNCS Transactions on
Computational Systems Biology –
Editorial Board

Table of Contents

Bio-inspired Network-Centric Operation and Control for Sensor/Actuator Networks

Falko Dressler

Autonomic Networking Group, Dept. of Computer Science 7,
University of Erlangen-Nuremberg, Germany
dressler@informatik.uni-erlangen.de,
http://www7.informatik.uni-erlangen.de/~dressler/

Abstract. Self-organization mechanisms have been investigated and developed to efficiently operate networked embedded systems. Special focus was given to wireless sensor networks (WSN) and sensor/actuator networks (SANET). Looking at the most pressing issues in such networks, the limited resources and the huge amount of interoperating nodes, the proposed solutions primarily intend to solve the scalability problems by reducing the overhead in data communication. Well-known examples are data-centric routing approaches and probabilistic techniques. In this paper, we intend to go one step further. We are about to also move the operation and control for WSN and SANET into the network. Inspired by the operation of complex biological systems such as the cellular information exchange, we propose a network-centric approach. Our method is based on three concepts: data-centric operation, specific reaction on received data, and simple local behavior control using a policy-based state machine. In summary, these mechanisms lead to an emergent system behavior that allows to control the operation of even large-scale sensor/actuator networks.

1 Introduction

In the communications area, there is a strong research focus on networked embedded systems because of their broad diversity in application domains. Especially, wireless sensor networks (WSN) have become popular for many applications. Similarly, there is a growing demand for sensor/actuator networks (SANET).

Sensor networks are composed of numerous small, independently operating sensor nodes [1]. Such sensors nodes are self-contained units consisting of a battery, radio communication, sensors, and some minimal amount of on board computing power. While the application scenarios are manifold [2], the operation of such WSNs is still challenging [3], basically due to the limited resources in terms of CPU power, storage, and, first of all, energy [4]. Within a WSN, nodes are thought to be deployed, to adapt to the environment, and to transmit data among themselves and/or to a given base station. The research topics include efficient communication in terms of resource consumption, reliability, and scalability [2,5]. Because sensor nodes are usually battery operated, many efforts

C. Priami (Ed.): Trans. on Comput. Syst. Biol. VIII, LNBI 4780, pp. 1–13, 2007.

have been made to develop energy-efficient algorithms and protocols for communication in WSNs [6].

Usually, WSNs are thought to be dynamic in terms of the current availability, i.e. they care about the potential removal and addition of sensor nodes. Dynamics in terms of mobility is concerned in sensor/actuator networks. Basically, SANETs consist of sensor networks that are enhanced by additional actuation facilities [3]. In most application scenarios, mobile robot systems are used as actuation facilities [7]. Nevertheless, we concentrate on general purpose actuation controlled by measures from corresponding sensor nodes. Therefore, the same network infrastructure is used for actuation control as well as for sensor data collection.

There are many application scenarios for WSNs and SANETs. The most popular examples include the service as first responders in emergency situations [8] and the supervision and control of challenging environments such as the monitoring of animals [9].

Operation and control of such networks is one of the most challenging issues. Typically, a central control loop is employed consisting of the following actions: measurement, transmission to a base station, (external) analysis, transmission to the actuation devices, actuation. Besides the increased network load, severe delays might be introduced. Driven by the limited resources, mechanisms for network self-organization have been proposed for higher scalability. Most of these approaches focus on efficient communication in WSNs, e.g. directed diffusion as a data-centric communication paradigm [10], and on stateless task allocation in SANETs [11]. Similar issues have been addressed in the artificial intelligence domain. Agent-based systems have been developed that enable an efficient distributed control in uncertain environments [12]. Nevertheless, there are still many unsolved issues such as predictability of an action, reliability of the communication, and boundaries for response times.

In this paper, we present and discuss an approach for *network-centric operation and control* in WSNs and SANETs that prevents the necessity of the described control loop or reduces the loop to a few neighboring nodes within the network, respectively. Inspired by the information handling in cell biology, we have built a rule-based system that allows to achieve all decisions within the network itself. There is no external control required. Nevertheless, we propose to allow such external intelligence for the handling of unexpected situations. The adaptive rule system has the inherent property of being self-learning by inducing new rules that match previously unknown situations. Therefore, our method provides at least limited control in a system showing an emergent behavior.

The network-centric control system allows to operate even in scenarios with the following challenging properties:

- Mobility of nodes – commonly it is believed that sensor networks being stationary, nowadays, mobility is a mayor concern
- Size of the network – much larger than in a infrastructure networks
- Density of deployment – very high, application domain dependent
- Energy constraints – much more stringent than in fixed or cellular networks, in certain cases the recharging of the energy source is impossible

The main contributions of the paper can be summarized as follows. An approach is presented that features localized data analysis and diffuse communication of measurement and computation results based on the content of the information instead of topology information and central management. We adapted signaling pathways known from cell biology to achieve an emergent behavior of the addressed complex system consisting of sensors and actuators. Using simple rules that are pre-programmed into network nodes, the network becomes able to solve aggregation or decision problems without having a global view to the behavior of the entire system.

The rest of the paper is organized as follows. Section 2 depicts the shifting paradigms to network-centric operation and control in massively distributed sensor/actuator networks. In section 3, the rule-based state machine for localized actuation control is explained. This description is followed by a discussion in section 4 and a conclusion in section 5.

2 Shifting Paradigms: Network-Centric Operation and Control

The objective of this paper is to discuss the potentials of network-centric control and operation in sensor/actuator networks. We developed a scheme based on three principles: data-centric operation, specific reaction on received data, and simple local behavior control using a policy-based state machine. We start with a high-level motivation for the presented approach, followed by a detailed description of the involved algorithms, and a discussion that is meant to be a starting point for further contemplation.

2.1 Need for Network-Centric Control

The coordination and control of sensor/actuator networks is still an emerging research area. Sensor networks have been enhanced by mobile robots. The resulting system is continuously examining the environment using sensors (measurement). The measurement data is transmitted to a (more or less) central system for further processing, e.g. optimizations using global state information. Then, the actuators are controlled by explicit commands that are finally executed (actuation). Basically, this scheme is usually used because the involved components (sensors, actuators) do not have resources that allow to cover the global state. The scheme is depicted in figure 1 (left). The measurement and the control loop are shown by corresponding arrows. Obviously, long transmission distances have to be bridged leading to unnecessarily high transmission delays as well as to a questionable communication overhead in the network, i.e. possible network congestion and energy wastage.

The favored behavior is shown in figure 1 (right). Self-organization methodologies are used to provide a network-centric actuation control, i.e. a processing of measurement data within the network and a direct interaction with associated, i.e. co-located actuators. How can we build a system that behaves in this fashion

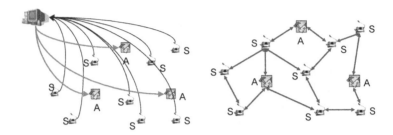

Fig. 1. Operation and control of a SANET: centralized (left), network-centric (right)

and that shows the desired emergent behavior? We tried to adapt mechanisms as known from cell biology as described in the next section. The result is a data-centric message forwarding, aggregation, and processing. The key requirements can be summarized as follows:

– Self-organized operation without central control
– Allowance for centralized "helpers" and self-learning properties
– Reduced network utilization
– Accelerated response, i.e. in-time actuation

2.2   An Excursion to Nature - Cellular Signaling Pathways

The turn to nature for solutions to technological questions has brought us many unforeseen great concepts. This encouraging course seems to hold on for many aspects in technology. Many efforts were made in the area of computer technology employing mechanisms known from biological systems [13]. For this work, we concentrate on information transmission and reaction capabilities employed by signaling pathways for inter-cellular communication [14].

The focus of this section is to briefly introduce the information exchange in cellular environments and to extract the issues in computer networks that can be addressed by the utilization of these mechanisms [15, 16]. Similar to the structure, the intercommunication within both systems is comparable [17, 18]. Information exchange between cells, called signaling pathways, follows the same principles that are required by network nodes. A message is sent to a destination and transferred, possibly using multiple hops, to this target.

From a local point of view, the information transfer works as follows. The cell expresses a specific surface molecule, the receptor. In consequence this receptor is activated, e.g. by a change in its sterical or chemical conformation (phosphorylation of defined amino acids). The activated receptor molecule is able to further activate intracellular molecules resulting in a "domino effect". The principle is not as simple as described here. Many of these signaling pathways are interfering and interacting. Different signaling molecules are affecting the same pathway. Inhibitory pathways are interfering with the straightforward signal transduction. To sum up, the final effect is dependent on the strongest signal. The effect of

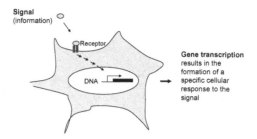

Fig. 2. Information exchange in the cellular environment

such a signal transduction pathway is mostly gene transcription, other possibilities are the reorganization of intracellular structure such as the cell cytoskeleton or the internalization and externalization in and out of the cell. Gene transcription means that the cell respond to incoming the signal by production of other factors which are then secreted (transported out of the cell), where it can induce signaling processes in the cell's direct environment. This process is depicted in a simplified manner in figure 2. A cell is shown with a single receptor that is able to receive a very specific signal, i.e. a protein, and to activate a signaling cascade which finally forms the cellular response.

This *specific response* is the key to information processing. It depends on the type of the signal and the state of the cells (which receptors have been built and which of them are already occupied by particular proteins). Finally, a specific cellular response is induced: either the local state is manipulated and/or a new messaging protein is created. The remote information exchange works analogue. Proteins, peptides, and steroids are used as information particles (hormones) between cells. A signal is released into the blood stream, the medium that carries it to distant cells and induces an answer in these cells which then passes on the information or can activate helper cells (e.g. the Renin-Angiotensin-Aldosteron system [19] and the immune system). The interesting property of this transmission is that the information itself addresses the destination. During differentiation a cell is programmed to express a subset of receptor in order to fulfill a specific function in the tissue. In consequence, hormones in the bloodstream affect only those cells expressing the correct receptor. This is the main reason for the specificity of cellular signal transduction. Of course, cells also express a variety of receptors which regulate the cellular metabolism, survival, and death.

The lessons to learn from biology are the efficient and, above all, the very specific response to a problem, the shortening of information pathways, and the possibility of directing each problem to the adequate helper component. Therefore, the adaptation of mechanisms from cell and molecular biology promises to enable a more efficient information exchange. Besides all the encouraging properties, bio-inspired techniques must be used carefully by modeling biological and technical systems and choosing only adequate solutions.

So, how to use the described methods to WSN and SANET operation and control? The biological model needs to be checked and - partially - adapted

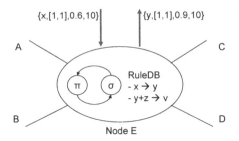

Fig. 3. Architecture and behavior of a local node

to match the tasks in sensor/actuator networks. In the following section, we describe and discuss a solution for network-centric operation and control based on the described biological mechanisms.

3   Rule-Based State Machine for Localized Actuation Control

As already mentioned, three basic mechanisms are used to achieve the demanded goals:

- *Data-centric operation* – Each message carries all necessary information to allow the specific handling of the associated data.
- *Specific reaction on received data* – A rule-based programming scheme is used to describe specific actions to be taken after the reception of particular information fragments.
- *Simple local behavior control* – We do not intend to control the overall system but focus on the operation of the individual node instead (see discussion on emergent system behavior in section 4). We designed simple state machines that control each node whether sensor or actuator.

The complete scheme as adapted from cellular behavior is shown in figure 3. Even though the principles are described later, the general architecture and the behavior can be shortly explained. Depicted is a network node that has four directly connected neighbors (A, B, C, D). The local behavior is controlled by a state machine (π, σ) and a set of rules (RuleDB). In this example, a data message of type x is received and transformed locally into a message of type y. Finally, this message is distributed to all neighbors. (Remark: we consider wireless communication. Therefore, each message that a node sends is basically a broadcast to all neighboring nodes.)

3.1   Data-Centric Operation

Classically, communication in ad hoc networks is based on topology information, i.e. routing paths that have been set-up prior to any data exchange. Additionally, each node carries a unique address that is used to distinguish the desired destination. We follow the approach used in typical data-centric communication schemes, e.g. directed diffusion [10], and replace topology information and addressing by data-centric operation. Each message is encoded as follows:

M:={type, region, confidence, content}

Using this description, we can encode measurement data as well as actuator information (type and content). Additionally, the region is included to distinguish messages from the local neighborhood from those that traveled over a long distance. Finally, the confidence value is used to evaluate the message in terms of importance or priority. Measures with a high confidence will have a stronger impact on calculations that those with a lower confidence. The confidence can be changed using aggregation schemes, i.e. two measures of the same value in the same region will lead to a higher confidence.

The following examples demonstrate the capabilities of the message encoding for data-centric operation:

- {temperatureC, [10,20], 0.6, 20} :: A temperature of 20C was measured at the coordinates [10,20]. The confidence is 0.6, therefore, a low-quality sensor was employed.
- {pictureJPG, [10,30], 0.9, "binary JPEG"} :: A picture was taken in format JPEG at the coordinates [10,30].

3.2   Specific Reaction on Received Data

An extensible and flexible rule system is used to evaluate received messages and to provide the "programming" that specifies the cellular response. Even though the message handling in biological cells is more sophisticated, the basic principles including the processing instructions (the DNA) are modeled. Each rule consists of two parts: a number of input values and some output: INPUT → OUTPUT. Therefore, typical rules could look like that:

- $A \rightarrow B$ :: message A is converted to message B
- $C \rightarrow \{\}$ :: message C is discarded
- $A \wedge B \rightarrow C$ :: if both messages A and B were received, a message C is created

Using all the other information available in each message, more complex rules can be derived:

- $A(\text{content} > 10) \rightarrow A(\text{confidence}:= 0.9)$ :: if the measured value was larger than 10, a copy of A is created with confidence set to 0.9
- $A(\text{content} = x) \wedge A(\text{content} = y) \rightarrow A(\text{content}:= x + y)$ :: two messages of type A are aggregated to a single one by adding their values

Again, an example is provided to reflect the capabilities of the data-centric operation:

- temperatureC(content> 85) →alarmFire(confidence:= 0.8)

Fig. 4. Simple state machines for sensors (S) and actuators (A)

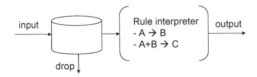

Fig. 5. Rule interpreter with system input and output

3.3   Simple Local Behavior Control

The local behavior is controlled by simple state machines acting as sensors or actuators. Additionally, an interpreter is checking the installed rules to previously received messages. It uses a queuing subsystem that acts as a generic receptor for all messages and keeps them for a given time. This time control is necessary to prevent queue overflows due to received messages of unknown type. The basic state machines for sensing and transmitting data and receiving and acting on data for sensors and actuators, respectively, are shown in figure 4.

The rule interpreter and its queuing system are depicted in figure 5. Basically, this is the standard behavior of each communication system. Received messages are stored in a local database. After a given timeout, each message is dropped in order to keep the size of the database below a given threshold. Periodically, the rule interpreter compares all received messages against the programmed rule set. A matching rule terminates the search and the rule is applied.

3.4   Case Studies

Two case studies are provided in this section to elaborate the principles and the flexibility of the proposed network-centric operation and control method for sensor/actuator networks: first, data aggregation and emergency calls, and secondly, in-network actuation control. Both examples were also chosen in order to show the benefits of our approach compared to traditional WSN mechanisms.

Data aggregation and emergency calls. We consider a typical scenario for wireless sensor networks. Sensor nodes are distributed over a given area. All nodes are equipped with sensors measuring a particular physical phenomenon, e.g. the temperature. In order to obtain information about the territory, the measurement results are transported to a given sink that analyzes the received temperature information. Additionally, measures exceeding a given threshold represent emergency situations that must be handled separately. In both examples, we assume a priority-based message forwarding scheme on the network layer.

1. Data types

$M_{temp} :=$ {temperature, position, content, priority}
$M_{alarm} :=$ {alarm, position, content, priority}

Examples:
 − {temperature, [10.5, 4.89], 26, 0.1}
 − {alarm, [0.8, 10.0], 75, 0.8}

2. Rule set

Aggregation:
$A_{temp}(content)eqB_{temp}(content) \rightarrow C_{temp}(priority := priority_A + (1 - priority_A) * priority_B)$
Emergency:
$A_{temp}(content > 70) \rightarrow B_{alarm}(priority := max(priority, 0.8)$

The aggregation rule combines multiple messages containing the same measurement results into a single message. Such aggregated messages must be handles with more care in the network since a packet loss of an aggregate of n messages can be compared to n separate lost packets without aggregation. In our example, the priority of the aggregated message is increased in order to enable the network layer to handle this packet specifically. The emergency rule creates new alarm packets if measurements above 70 degrees were observed. Additionally, the priority is explicitly set to a high value representing the importance of such a message.

3. Evaluation

The benefits of the aggregation and emergency example can be shown easily. Consider the following scenario. All sensor nodes are directly connected to a central base station. In this case, each message must travel exactly one hop before processing. There is no possibility for aggregation to take place. In every other case, multi hop communication is involved and multiple messages can be aggregated. Compared to a pure central processing, the approach always leads to a noticeable reduction of the network load.

In-network actuation control. A second example includes additional actuators. Based on the temperature measurement as discussed before, temperature control should be performed, e.g. by using AC or heatings. Such actuators are controlled by special control messages. In the following description, only the differences and additions to the previous example are shown.

1. Data types

   $M_{control} := \{control, position, delta, priority\}$

   Examples:
   - $\{control, [10.0, 10.0], +5, 0.1\}$
   - $\{control, [1.0, 10.0], -10, 0.8\}$

2. Rule set

   Control$_1$: $A_{temp}(content! = 20) \rightarrow B_{control}(delta := 20 - content_A)$
   Control$_2$: $A_{control} \rightarrow$ execute actuation command

   Two types of control rules exist. The first one (Control$_1$) can be seen as the in-network processing part. Received messages are verified whether actuation control should take place. In our example, a mean temperature of 20 degrees should be maintained. The second rule (Control$_2$) depicts the actuation initiation. After receiving a control message at an actuator, it performs the necessary actuation as encoded in the message (after checking if it can provide the needed service).

3. Evaluation

   Similarly to the previous example, a fully connected network (all sensors and actuators have a direct connection to the base station) will always perform optimal in terms of network overhead. Nevertheless, such a topology is unrealistic considering larger areas to be observed and maintained. In this case, each sensor message must traverse a multi hop path toward the base station. Then, after a meaningful evaluation, the actuation control must travel back to the actuators.

   In this case study, another possible topology can be imagined that also leads to a non-optimal operation of the proposed solution: if all sensors build a separate network partition as well as all actuators, then the base station will become the gateway between both networks. In this case all messages must traverse the base, i.e. there is no overhead in terms of duplicate network utilization for sensor and actuation control messages. Admittedly, this scenario is unrealistic as well.

   In conclusion, our solution for network-centric operation and control will perform at least as good as a central base station approach and outperform it in most realistic network scenarios, i.e. in networks consisting of a mixture of sensors and actuators.

4 Discussion

Based on the previously stated key requirements, the benefits of the proposed solution are reviewed in the following. Additionally, potential disadvantages or problems are stated and discussed:

- Self-organized operation without central control – The presented approach is based on locally available information only. Using the flexible rule system, arbitrary data-centric operations can be defined enabling the systems to specifically act on each received message.
- Allowance for centralized "helpers" and self-learning properties – Rules can be specified to forward all unknown messages to a central "helper". This system can examine the message, create according rules, and submit these rules to replace/enhance the rules installed in the SANET nodes. Therefore, our method provides at least limited control in a system showing an emergent behavior.
- Reduced network utilization – The network utilization no longer depends on the amount of measurement data to be transmitted to a base station. Instead, the rule system is responsible if and how messages have to be forwarded to more distant regions of the network.
- Accelerated response / actuation – The response time is much smaller than in the centralized approach due to the shortened data paths from measurement to processing, which takes place directly within the network, and the actuation. Depending on the installed rules and their spatial distribution, even boundaries for the response time can be derived.

Potential problems can appear through the inherent characteristics of such self-organizing processes [20], i.e. issues such as predictability of an action, reliability of the communication, and boundaries for response times must be considered. In general, there is no global state information available. Therefore, optimal solutions for the entire network cannot be calculated based on all theoretically available measures. Nevertheless, depending on the rule set, solutions can be derived that approximate the globally optimal solution quite well. Another issue is the necessary pre-programming of the rule sets into all the nodes. If new algorithms should be deployed, which is easy and straightforward using a central control, all or at least many of the distributed nodes must be changed. Fortunately, there are already network-based reprogramming techniques [21] and robot-assisted solutions [22] available to provide this functionality.

5   Conclusion

In this paper, we presented and discussed a methodology for network-centric operation and control of sensor/actuator networks. Inspired by biological information processing, we developed three easy to handle building blocks: data-centric communication, a state machine, and a rule-based decision process. Using these algorithms, the handling and processing of sensor data within the network itself becomes possible. In particular, we demonstrated that a collaborative sensing and processing approach for sensor/actuator networks based on local intelligence is possible. The interaction and collaboration between these nodes finally leads to an optimized system behavior in an emergent way.

Further work is needed in two directions: first, a detailed performance analysis for different application scenarios is necessary in order to rate the practical usability of the approach depending on the scenario. Secondly, it might be helpful if the rule sets are not "programmed" into each node but exchanged and updated on-demand by the nodes themselves in terms of a learning process.

Acknowledgments

The conducted research on bio-inspired networking is collaborative work with Dr. B. Krüger, Dept. of Physiology, University of Erlangen-Nuremberg, Germany.

References

1. Estrin, D., Culler, D., Pister, K., Sukhatme, G.S.: Connecting the Physical World with Pervasive Networks. IEEE Pervasive Computing 1, 59–69 (2002)
2. Akyildiz, I.F., Su, W., Sankarasubramaniam, Y., Cayirci, E.: A Survey on Sensor Networks. IEEE Communications Magazine 40, 102–116 (2002)
3. Akyildiz, I.F., Kasimoglu, I.H.: Wireless Sensor and Actor Networks: Research Challenges. Elsevier Ad Hoc Network Journal 2, 351–367 (2004)
4. Margi, C.: A Survey on Networking, Sensor Processing and System Aspects of Sensor Networks. Report, University of California, Santa Cruz (2003)
5. Culler, D., Estrin, D., Srivastava, M.B.: Overview of Sensor Networks. Computer 37, 41–49 (2004)
6. Chong, C.-Y., Kumar, S.P.: Sensor Networks: Evolution, Opportunities, and Challenges. Proceedings of the IEEE 91, 1247–1256 (2003)
7. Parker, L.E.: Current Research in Multi-Robot System. Journal of Artificial Life and Robotics 7 (2004)
8. Kumar, V., Rus, D., Singh, S.: Robot and Sensor Networks for First Responders. IEEE Pervasive Computing 3, 24–33 (2004)
9. Mainwaring, A., Polastre, J., Szewczyk, R., Culler, D., Anderson, J.: Wireless Sensor Networks for Habitat Monitoring. In: First ACM Workshop on Wireless Sensor Networks and Applications, Atlanta, GA, USA, ACM Press, New York (2002)
10. Intanagonwiwat, C., Govindan, R., Estrin, D.: Directed diffusion: A scalable and robust communication paradigm for sensor networks. In: 6th Annual ACM/IEEE International Conference on Mobile Computing and Networking (MobiCOM'00), Boston, MA, USA, pp. 56–67. IEEE Computer Society Press, Los Alamitos (2000)
11. Batalin, M.A., Sukhatme, G.S.: Using a Sensor Network for Distributed Multi-Robot Task Allocation. In: IEEE International Conference on Robotics and Automation, New Orleans, LA, USA, May 2003, pp. 158–164. IEEE Computer Society Press, Los Alamitos (2003)
12. Muscettola, N., Nayak, P.P., Pell, B., Williams, B.C.: Remote Agent: To Boldly Go Where No AI System Has Gone Before. Artificial Intelligence 100, 5–48 (1998)
13. Eigen, M., Schuster, P.: The Hypercycle: A Principle of Natural Self Organization. Springer, Berlin (1979)
14. Dressler, F.: Efficient and Scalable Communication in Autonomous Networking using Bio-inspired Mechanisms - An Overview. Informatica - An International Journal of Computing and Informatics 29, 183–188 (2005)
15. Alberts, B., Bray, D., Lewis, J., Raff, M., Roberts, K., Watson, J.D.: Molecular Biology of the Cell, 3rd edn. Garland Publishing, Inc. (1994)

16. Pawson, T.: Protein modules and signalling networks. Nature 373, 573–580 (1995)
17. Dressler, F., Krüger, B.: Cell biology as a key to computer networking. In: German Conference on Bioinformatics 2004 (GCB'04), Poster Session, Bielefeld, Germany (2004)
18. Krüger, B., Dressler, F.: Molecular Processes as a Basis for Autonomous Networking. IPSI Transactions on Advances Research: Issues in Computer Science and Engineering 1, 43–50 (2005)
19. Guyton, A.: Blood pressure control - special role of the kidneys and body fluids. Science 252, 1813–1816 (1991)
20. Prehofer, C., Bettstetter, C.: Self-Organization in Communication Networks: Principles and Design Paradigms. IEEE Communications Magazine 43, 78–85 (2005)
21. Jeong, J., Culler, D.: Incremental Network Programming for Wireless Sensors. In: First IEEE International Conference on Sensor and Ad hoc Communications and Networks (IEEE SECON), IEEE Computer Society Press, Los Alamitos (2004)
22. Fuchs, G., Truchat, S., Dressler, F.: Distributed Software Management in Sensor Networks using Profiling Techniques. In: 1st IEEE/ACM International Conference on Communication System Software and Middleware (IEEE COMSWARE 2006): 1st International Workshop on Software for Sensor Networks (SensorWare 2006), New Dehli, India, ACM Press, New York (2006)

A Computationally Fast and Parametric Model to Estimate Protein-Ligand Docking Time for Stochastic Event Based Simulation

Preetam Ghosh, Samik Ghosh, Kalyan Basu, and Sajal K. Das

Biological Networks (BONE) Research Group, Dept. of Comp. Sc. & Engg.
The University of Texas at Arlington, TX, USA
{ghosh, sghosh, basu, das}@cse.uta.edu

Abstract. This paper presents a computationally fast analytical model to estimate the time taken for protein-ligand docking in biological pathways. The environment inside the cell has been reported to be unstable with a considerable degree of randomness creating a stochastic resonance. To facilitate the understanding of the dynamic behavior of biological systems, we propose an "in silico" stochastic event based simulation. The implementation of this simulation requires the computation of the *execution times* of different biological events such as the protein-ligand docking process (time required for ligand-protein binding) as a *random variable*. The next event time of the system is computed by adding the event execution time to the clock value of the event start time. Our mathematical model takes special consideration of the actual biological process of ligand-protein docking with emphasis on the structural configurations of the ligands, proteins and the binding mechanism that enable us to control the model parameters considerably. We use a modification of the collision theory based approach to capture the randomness of this problem in discrete time and estimate the first two moments of this process. The numerical results for the first moment show promising correspondence with experimental results and demonstrate the efficacy of our model.

1   Introduction

The Genome project [1], tremendous advancement in micro-array analysis techniques [2], and large scale assay technologies like cDNA array [3] are generating large volumes of scientific data for biological systems, from microbes to homosapiens. We are now in an era where our capability of generating relevant data is less of an obstacle than our understanding of biological systems or networks. The system simulation of biological processes is now considered an important technique to understand its dynamics. The concept of "in silico" [4,5,6] or discrete event based modeling has been successfully applied to study many complex systems. Our goal is to build a similar discrete event based framework for complex biological systems [9,12]. Our main motivation is to overcome the complexities of current mesoscale and stochastic simulation methods and create a flexible simulation

C. Priami (Ed.): Trans. on Comput. Syst. Biol. VIII, LNBI 4780, pp. 14–41, 2007.
© Springer-Verlag Berlin Heidelberg 2007

framework. The mesoscale model deals with rate equation based kinetic models and uses continuous time deterministic techniques. Such model is closely related to a rate constant derived from measurements, which captures the experimental boundary conditions and physical reaction dynamics. This model solves complex differential equations corresponding to chemical reactions using numerical integration. Numerical integrations are normally computed at 10^{-6} time steps i.e., the instruction set for each equation is computed every microsecond. The current super scalar computers with dual processors can compute around $2-3$ machine instructions per clock cycle. Thus the maximum number of instructions that can be supported per microsecond is about $2000-3000$ with a 1 GHZ clock. This might not be sufficient to solve a system of even 1000 equations (25 machine instructions per equation results in a > 10 times speed reduction). Since a biological system involves a very large number of differential equations (> 1000), the mesoscale model is not suitable for a large system. Also the stochastic resonance [13] specially for protein creation and other signaling pathways are not properly captured in the mesoscale model unless it is modified to the stochastic mode. The Stochastic simulation models are based on rate equations, namely Gillespie technique [14] and its variations such as Kitano's Cell Designer [15], DARPA's BioSpice [16], StochSim [17], Cell Illustrator [18] etc. and it has more computational overhead due to the random number computations at each time step. Due to the large number of protein complexes in a cell, these models lead to combinatorial explosion in the number of reactions, thus making them unmanageable for complex signaling pathway problems. These limitations of current techniques and the potential opportunity to integrate multi-layer events under one simulation framework motivates our work.

Fig 1 presents an overview of our multi-scale discrete event based framework. We define a biological network/system as a collection of cells which are in turn a collection of biological processes. Each process comprises a number of functions, where a function will be modeled as an event. A unique pathway will be defined as a biological process consisting of a number of biological functions. The fundamental entity in our proposed mathematical model is an "event" which represents a biological function with relevant boundary conditions. These event models are then used to develop a stochastic discrete-event simulation. The interactions between cells are captured in the Biological network view. Then for every cell all the biological processes are identified and their relationship is defined in the cell view of the biological system. Each pathway is described by the event diagram of the biological process. There is a considerable amount of pathway information currently captured in different bioinformatics databases [17],[37],[38]. Thus the completion of these event diagrams seem feasible now. All these events are statistically modeled using the functionality of that particular biological event. The mathematical abstraction of these events can be selected based on the complexity of the event dynamics and its mechanism. This flexibility of using different mathematical abstractions for different types of events make this technique more attractive than π-calculus [41,42,43,44] or other types of stochastic system modeling. This paper focuses on the modeling of one such event: 'ligand-protein'

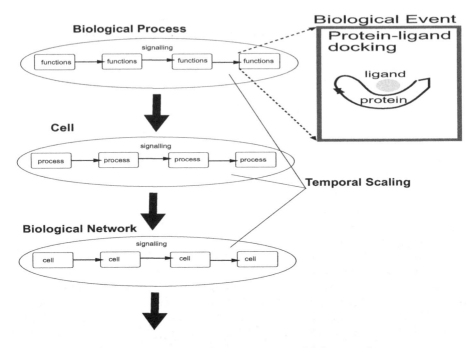

Fig. 1. Multi-scale discrete event model framework

docking. We present a parametric mathematical model to compute the execution time (or *holding time*) for ligand-protein binding (i.e., time required for the binding to occur) which is also computationally fast. We have already developed a few models for modeling other biological events like (1) cytoplasmic reactions [10][11], (2) Protein DNA binding [40] and (3) arrival of Mg^{2+} molecule signal from external cell environment to trigger a pathway [39].

1.1   Related Works

Most of the work on protein-ligand docking use Brownian dynamic simulations to model the mechanism. From the point of view of kinetics, protein docking should entail distinct kinetic regimes where different driving forces govern the binding process at different times [26,27,28]. This is because of the free energy funnel created by the binding site of the protein. The funnel distinguishes three kinetic regimes. First, nonspecific diffusion (regime I) brings the molecules to close proximity. This is the motion created by the random collision of the molecules. Second, in the recognition stage (regime II), the chemical affinity steers the molecules into relatively well oriented encounter complexes ($\approx 5 \times 10^{-10}$ m), overcoming the mostly entropic barrier to binding. Brownian dynamics simulation of this regime [19] were also found to be consistent with a significant narrowing of the binding pathway to the final bound conformation. Finally, regime III corresponds to the docking stage where short-range forces mold the high affinity interface of the complex structure.

Long-range electrostatic effects can heavily bias the approach of the molecules to favor reactive conditions. This effect was shown to be important for many association processes, including those of proteins with DNA [8], proteins with highly charged small molecules [29], and proteins with oppositely charged protein substrates [30,31,32,33,34]. These systems have been thoroughly studied, and are frequently regarded as typical examples of binding phenomena. Electrostatics is clearly not the only force that can affect the association rate. In addition to electrostatics, the most important process contributing to the binding free energy is desolvation, i.e., the removal of solvent both from nonpolar (hydrophobic) and polar atoms [35]. It is generally accepted that partial desolvation is always a significant contribution to the free energy in protein-protein association, and it becomes dominant for complexes in which the long-range electrostatic interactions are weak [36]. Brownian dynamics simulations to study the effects of desolvation on the rates of diffusion-limited protein-protein association have been reported in [19].

In this paper, our goal is to introduce a collision theory model to explain the temporal kinetics of ligand-protein docking. This is a simplified model which does not incorporate the effects of electrostatic forces and desolvation directly as parameters of the model but consider their effects through the random molecular motion of the proteins in the binding environment. This simplification of the model makes it a random collision problem within the cell and gives us a fairly accurate but computationally fast model for the docking time estimate to be used by our stochastic simulator. Note that the Gillespie simulator considers the docking process as another rate-based equation (a measured quantity that encapsulates all the kinetic properties of the process during the experiment), whereas our proposed model can incorporate the salient features of the docking process along with the structural and functional properties of the protein-ligand pair. This parametric presentation of the binding process makes the model generic in nature and can be easily used for other cases of protein-ligand binding where the assumptions are valid. The results generated by this model are very close to experimental estimates. The main conclusion of our work is that the total time required for docking is mostly contributed by the repeated collisions of the ligand with the protein. Also because the ligand on arriving inside the cell compartment spends most of the time (for binding) away from the protein (to which it binds), the effects of electrostatic force and desolvation are negligible in the binding time estimation. However, they play a significant role in the determination of the free energy change of the docked complex [19] which in turn is used in determining the probability of docking as stated later in the paper.

2 Analytical Model: Ligand-Protein Docking

Let us consider the docking between a protein A and a ligand B. Let the total number of surface binding points in A be n_A and that in B be n_B. The number of surface docking points to produce the AB complex is denoted by n_s, such that:

$$n_s << n_A; \quad n_s << n_B \tag{1}$$

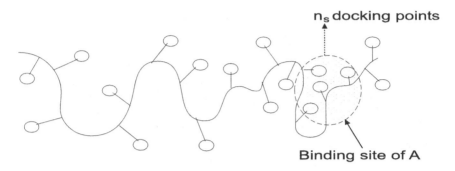

Protein A

Fig. 2. The protein docking mechanism

We assume that the n_s docking points are all contiguous. We also assume that if any *three* of the docking points is hit by the ligand during a collision, the attractive force of the amino acid side-chain will force the ligand to change orientation so that it can bind to the site. This assumption has a few limitations which we will discuss in Section 5. Now, let the total probability of hitting the site during a collision for successful docking be p_f. The probability of hitting the binding site at only one of the docking points is $p_f^1 = \frac{\binom{n_s}{1}}{\binom{n_A}{1}\binom{n_B}{1}}$. Similarly, the probability of hitting the binding site at i docking points is given by:

$$p_f^i = \frac{\binom{n_s}{i}}{\binom{n_A}{i}\binom{n_B}{i}}, \quad (1 \le i \le n_s) \tag{2}$$

Thus p_f can be expressed as follows:

$$p_f = \sum_{i=3}^{n_s} p_f^i = \sum_{i=1}^{n_s} \frac{\binom{n_s}{i}}{\binom{n_A}{i}\binom{n_B}{i}} \tag{3}$$

Also, let p_b denote the probability that the ligand collides with the protein A with sufficient kinetic energy for successful docking. Hence, the total probability that the ligand hits the binding site while colliding with the protein, p_t, is given by:

$$p_t = p_b \times p_f \tag{4}$$

In general, the process of protein-ligand association can be described by a three-step reaction mechanism as follows:

$$A + B = \Longleftrightarrow_{k^-}^{k^+} A...B \Longleftrightarrow_{k_1^-}^{k_1^+} A - B \Longleftrightarrow_{k_{AB}^-}^{k_{AB}^+} AB, \tag{5}$$

where $A...B$ denotes the nonspecific encounter pairs, $A-B$ denotes the precursor state(s) leading to the docked conformation AB [20]. If long-range interactions can be neglected, the first reaction step is the random collision of the protein and ligand (A and B), resulting in a nonspecific encounter complex $A...B$ within the desolvation layer. To a good approximation, the limiting rate k^+ of this first regime is given by the Smoluchowski limit [21], k_{coll}. Indeed, the overall repulsion of the force fields has little effect on k^+. The authors in [19] report that the typical lifetime of a nonspecific encounter complex $A...B$ diffusing within the desolvation layer is about 4 ± 1 ns. This value is consistent with the nonspecific affinity between proteins that is estimated to be $10^2 M^{-1}$ or less [22].

The third reaction step in Eq. 5 i.e., the late transition between the favorable intermediate(s) $A - B$ and the bound state AB, substantially differs from the first two steps. The onset of the late transition coincides with the need to remove steric clashes and charge overlaps in the binding mechanism. Although the first two steps are governed by diffusion, the third is a process of induced fit that requires structural rearrangements involving mostly side chains. [19] reports that this late transition is not diffusive. For ligands that bind in a diffusion-controlled (or diffusion limited) reaction, the rate-limiting step must be the diffusive search for the partially desolvated intermediate(s) or precursor state(s) rather than the third step, and thus $k^+_{AB} \gg k^-_1$.

In this paper, we focus on the kinetics of the total binding process. In particular, the collision theory model incorporates the first two steps together, whereas the Ligand axis rotation model estimates the third step.

2.1   Rotation of the Ligand Axis with Respect to Protein A

Fig 3 shows the rotation of the ligand axis to bring about the final docking configuration. The final orientation can be reached by the rotation of the ligand

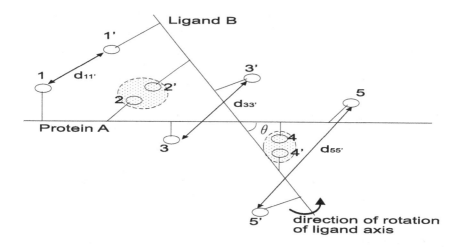

Fig. 3. The rotation of the ligand axis

axis by an angle θ, where $(0 \leq \theta \leq 2\pi)$. However, as we will see in Section 4, this angle is often quite small ranging between $(0 \leq \theta \leq \frac{\pi}{2})$. Also, we must have:

$$d_{11'} \leq \gamma, \quad d_{33'} \leq \gamma, \quad d_{55'} \leq \gamma \tag{6}$$

where, γ is the threshold distance between any two binding points of A and B respectively for docking to occur. Note that γ can be estimated from the structural properties of the protein/ligand interaction [45].

2.2 Assumptions

1. Only the ligand rotates, to reach the final docked conformation whereas the protein remains fixed. In particular, we consider the *relative rotation* of the ligand axis with respect to the protein axis.
2. The docking point extends out of the ligand/protein backbones at an angle to the corresponding axis. In the analytical model, we have included both the cases when this angle is equal to $\frac{\pi}{2}$ and otherwise. The subsequent numerical results have been generated assuming an angle equal to $\frac{\pi}{2}$ as this is not yet reflected in the biological databases.
3. The *docking site* on the ligand/protein backbones are approximated as straight lines for ease in calculations. Note that the first step is to find the average angle (in radians) that the binding site of the ligand axis has to rotate to reach the final docked conformation. We assume that the binding site of the ligand behaves like a rubber handle extending out of the spherical ligand structure. This allows us to compute the average time taken for the rotation of the ligand axis easily.
4. At least 3 docking points in the ligand has to come within the range of the threshold distance of the corresponding 3 docking points in protein A for a successful binding to occur.
5. We consider a 2-d coordinate system to estimate our results. A 3-d coordinate system can be used following the same concept but the equations become quite complicated to solve as discussed later. If 3 docking points are considered, it is always feasible to have the three points on the same plane where the other points are contributing to reduce the rotational threshold energy required for binding for these three 2-d points. Thus a 2-d assumption is appropriate for the model.
6. The docking points extend out of the protein/ligand backbones in a straight line.

The requirement of *at least 3 docking points* to come within the threshold distance of γ allows us to calculate the average angle of rotation, θ_{avg}, that the ligand axis has to rotate for successful docking with Protein A as discussed below.

2.3 Finding θ_{avg}

It should be noted that in the subsequent discussion all references to the ligand/protein backbones actually applies to only the docking site of the corresponding backbones (which are assumed as straight lines). Fig 4 shows the

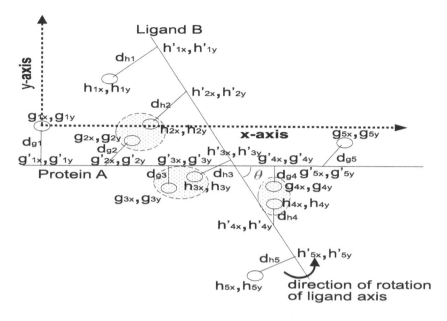

Fig. 4. Ligand and Protein coming within threshold distance of 3 docking points

scenario when the ligand and the protein come within a distance of γ for at least 3 docking points.

Conventions

1. There are a total of n_s docking points.
2. The docking points on the *protein* are labelled as (g_{ix}, g_{iy}) to denote the x and y coordinates respectively of the ith docking point.
3. The points on the amino acid backbone of the *protein* corresponding to the ith docking points are denoted by (g'_{ix}, g'_{iy}).
4. The docking points on the *ligand* are labelled as (h_{ix}, h_{iy}) to denote the x and y coordinates respectively of the ith docking point.
5. The points on the amino acid backbone of the *ligand* corresponding to the ith docking points are denoted by (h'_{ix}, h'_{iy}).
6. The origin of our 2-d coordinate system is at (g_{1x}, g_{1y}), i.e, $(g_{1x}, g_{1y}) = (0,0)$.
7. The distance between the ith docking point and the corresponding point on the *protein* backbone is given by d_{gi}.
8. The distance between the ith docking point and the corresponding point on the *ligand* backbone is given by d_{hi}.
9. The angle between the straight line connecting the ith docking point and the protein backbone and the straight line denoting the protein backbone is denoted by ϕ_i.
10. The angle between the straight line connecting the ith docking point and the ligand backbone and the straight line denoting the ligand backbone is denoted by ψ_i.

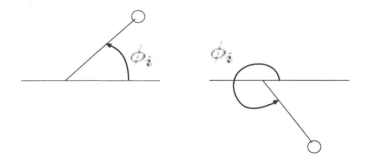

Fig. 5. Determining the angles between the axis and the docking point

11. The docking site on the protein backbone (assumed to be a straight line) is parallel to the x-axis of the 2-d coordinate system. Thus the equation of this straight line is $y = -(d_{g1}) \sin \phi_1$.
12. The distance between the points on the protein backbone corresponding to the ith and j^{th} docking points is denoted by D_{gij}.
13. The distance between the points on the ligand backbone corresponding to the ith and j^{th} docking points is denoted by D_{hij}.

The angles ϕ_i, $(\forall i)$ are measured from the protein axis to the straight line extending out of the axis carrying the docking point in an anti-clockwise direction as shown in Fig 5. Similarly, the angles ψ_i, $(\forall i)$ are also computed.

Calculating the coordinates of the docking points of the protein backbone. Its fairly easy to compute the coordinates of all the n_s docking points and their corresponding contact points on the protein backbone. We will simplistically sketch the process in this section.

The first docking point on the protein backbone, (g_{1x}, g_{1y}) is considered to be the origin of our coordinate system. Also, because the equation of the straight line denoting the protein axis is known, we can write:

$$(g_{1x}, g_{1y}) = (0, 0); \tag{7}$$

$$g'_{1y} = -(d_{g1}) \sin \phi_1; \quad (g'_{1x})^2 + (g'_{1y})^2 = (d_{g1})^2 \tag{8}$$

From, Eq 8 we can readily calculate (g'_{1x}, g'_{1y}). Next, we can compute (g'_{ix}, g'_{iy}), $(1 \leq i \leq n_s)$ by solving the following set of equations:

$$g'_{iy} = -(d_{g1}) \sin \phi_1 \tag{9}$$

$$(g'_{ix} - g'_{1x})^2 + (g'_{iy} - g'_{1y})^2 = (D_{g1i})^2; \quad 2 \leq i \leq n_s \tag{10}$$

Next, we can estimate the coordinates of the docking points of the protein (g_{ix}, g_{iy}), $(2 \leq i \leq n_s)$ by solving the following equation pair:

$$(g'_{ix} - g_{ix})^2 + (g'_{iy} - g_{iy})^2 = (d_{gi})^2; \quad g_{iy} = g'_{iy} + (d_{gi}) \sin \phi_i \tag{11}$$

Calculating the coordinates of any three docking points on the ligand.
The angle θ as shown in Fig 4 denotes the angle made by the docking sites of
the ligand backbone with the protein backbone (and equivalently the x-axis). As
mentioned before, we assume that *any three* docking points on the ligand come
within the threshold distance of the corresponding docking points of the protein.
Without loss of generality, let us assume that these 3 docking points are denoted
by (h_{ix}, h_{iy}), (h_{jx}, h_{jy}) and (h_{kx}, h_{ky}) corresponding to the docking points on
the protein denoted by (g_{ix}, g_{iy}), (g_{jx}, g_{jy}) and (g_{kx}, g_{ky}), where $1 \leq i, j, k \leq n_s$
and $i \neq j \neq k$. Thus we can write:

$$(h_{ix} - g_{ix})^2 + (h_{iy} - g_{iy})^2 \leq \gamma^2 \tag{12}$$

$$(h_{jx} - g_{jx})^2 + (h_{jy} - g_{jy})^2 \leq \gamma^2 \tag{13}$$

$$(h_{kx} - g_{kx})^2 + (h_{ky} - g_{ky})^2 \leq \gamma^2 \tag{14}$$

Next, we can find the distance between the docking points (h_{ix}, h_{iy}) and their
corresponding points of attachment to the ligand axis (h'_{ix}, h'_{iy}) denoted by d_{hi}
(from the PDB database [7]) and hence:

$$(h_{ix} - h'_{ix})^2 + (h_{iy} - h'_{iy})^2 = (d_{hi})^2 \tag{15}$$

$$(h_{jx} - h'_{jx})^2 + (h_{jy} - h'_{jy})^2 = (d_{hj})^2 \tag{16}$$

$$(h_{kx} - h'_{kx})^2 + (h_{ky} - h'_{ky})^2 = (d_{hk})^2 \tag{17}$$

The distances between the corresponding points on the ligand axis can also be
estimated (from the PDB database) and we have:

$$(h'_{ix} - h'_{jx})^2 + (h'_{iy} - h'_{jy})^2 = (D_{hij})^2 \tag{18}$$

$$(h'_{ix} - h'_{kx})^2 + (h'_{iy} - h'_{ky})^2 = (D_{hik})^2 \tag{19}$$

Also, our assumption that the docking points extend out of the ligand backbone
in a straight line allows us to formulate the slope of these lines as $\frac{h_{iy} - h'_{iy}}{h_{ix} - h'_{ix}}$,
$\frac{h_{jy} - h'_{jy}}{h_{jx} - h'_{jx}}$ and $\frac{h_{ky} - h'_{ky}}{h_{kx} - h'_{kx}}$. And because the corresponding angles of these lines with
the ligand axis can be estimated, we have:

$$\left\{
\begin{array}{ll}
\tan \psi_i = \dfrac{\frac{h_{iy} - h'_{iy}}{h_{ix} - h'_{ix}} - m}{1 + m \frac{h_{iy} - h'_{iy}}{h_{ix} - h'_{ix}}}, & \text{for } \psi_i \neq \frac{\pi}{2} \\[2em]
m \frac{h_{iy} - h'_{iy}}{h_{ix} - h'_{ix}} = -1, & \text{for } \psi_i = \frac{\pi}{2}
\end{array}
\right\} \tag{20}$$

$$\left\{
\begin{array}{ll}
\tan \psi_j = \dfrac{\frac{h_{jy} - h'_{jy}}{h_{jx} - h'_{jx}} - m}{1 + m \frac{h_{jy} - h'_{jy}}{h_{jx} - h'_{jx}}}, & \text{for } \psi_j \neq \frac{\pi}{2} \\[2em]
m \frac{h_{jy} - h'_{jy}}{h_{jx} - h'_{jx}} = -1, & \text{for } \psi_j = \frac{\pi}{2}
\end{array}
\right\} \tag{21}$$

$$\left\{
\begin{array}{ll}
\tan \psi_k = \dfrac{\frac{h_{ky} - h'_{ky}}{h_{kx} - h'_{kx}} - m}{1 + m \frac{h_{ky} - h'_{ky}}{h_{kx} - h'_{kx}}}, & \text{for } \psi_k \neq \frac{\pi}{2} \\[2em]
m \frac{h_{ky} - h'_{ky}}{h_{kx} - h'_{kx}} = -1, & \text{for } \psi_k = \frac{\pi}{2}
\end{array}
\right\} \tag{22}$$

where, m is the slope of the straight line denoting the ligand axis. Note that, in Section 4, we assume an angle of $\frac{\pi}{2}$ to generate the results as the corresponding angles are not reported in the biological databases. Finally, because the points (h'_{ix}, h'_{iy}), (h'_{jx}, h'_{jy}) and (h'_{kx}, h'_{ky}) lie on the same straight line (i.e, the ligand backbone), we can write:

$$h'_{ky} - h'_{iy} = (h'_{kx} - h'_{ix}) \frac{h'_{jy} - h'_{iy}}{h'_{jx} - h'_{ix}} \tag{23}$$

$$h'_{ky} - h'_{jy} = (h'_{kx} - h'_{jx}) \frac{h'_{jy} - h'_{iy}}{h'_{jx} - h'_{ix}} \tag{24}$$

Thus, in Equations 12-24, we have 13 equations to solve for the following 13 unknown variables: $h_{ix}, h_{iy}, h_{jx}, h_{jy}, h_{kx}, h_{ky}, h'_{ix}, h'_{iy}, h'_{jx}, h'_{jy}, h'_{kx}, h'_{ky}$ and m. Note that, we need at least 3 docking points to form sufficient number of equations for solving all the unknown variables. To calculate θ from m, we observe that the slope of the ligand axis is given by $\tan(\theta)$, such that we have:

$$\theta = \arctan(m) \tag{25}$$

Note that the slope can be both positive or negative resulting in clockwise or anticlockwise rotations of the ligand axis. However, because we are interested in computing the time for rotation of the ligand axis, the direction of rotation is not important for us. Also, because the equations are nonlinear and involve inequalities, we can only make an approximate estimate of the coordinates of the docking points on the ligand.

Calculating θ_{avg} from θ. The next step is to estimate the average angle of rotation, θ_{avg}. We will find the angle θ (as outlined above) considering any 3 docking points out of the possible n_s points. This requires a total of $\binom{n_s}{3}$ iterations.

We next find the average angle of rotation considering 3 docking points, θ_{avg}^3, from the $\binom{n_s}{3}$ different θ_i^3's ($1 \leq i \leq \binom{n_s}{3}$) calculated (where, θ_i^3 denotes the angle computed using the above equations for the ith combination of 3 docking points). Assuming uniform probability for all these cases, we have:

$$\theta_{avg}^3 = \sum_{i=1}^{\binom{n_s}{3}} \frac{\theta_i^3}{\binom{n_s}{3}} \tag{26}$$

Note that if greater number of docking points come within the threshold distance, θ_{avg}^j ($4 \leq j \leq n_s$) will continue to decrease. We next consider the case when more than 3 docking points come within the threshold distance. If 4 points come within the distance, we will have an extra 4 variables to solve ($h_{mx}, h_{my}, h'_{mx}, h'_{my}$). Note that our assumptions for this coordinate system is only valid if all of these four points are on the same plane. We will have another 4 equations by adding the equations corresponding to this new point to the Eqs 12-14, Eqs 15-17, Eqs 18-19 and Eqs 20-22 respectively as follows:

$$(h_{mx} - g_{mx})^2 + (h_{my} - g_{my})^2 = \gamma^2 \tag{27}$$

$$(h_{mx} - h'_{mx})^2 + (h_{my} - h'_{my})^2 = (d_{hm})^2 \tag{28}$$

$$(h'_{ix} - h'_{mx})^2 + (h'_{iy} - h'_{my})^2 = (D_{him})^2 \tag{29}$$

$$\left\{ \begin{array}{l} \tan \psi_m = \dfrac{\frac{h_{my} - h'_{my}}{h_{mx} - h'_{mx}} - m}{1 + m \frac{h_{my} - h'_{my}}{h_{mx} - h'_{mx}}}, \quad \text{for } \psi_m \neq \frac{\pi}{2} \\[3ex] m \dfrac{h_{my} - h'_{my}}{h_{mx} - h'_{mx}} = -1, \quad \text{for } \psi_m = \frac{\pi}{2} \end{array} \right\} \tag{30}$$

Next we can calculate the average angle of rotation considering 4 docking points, θ^4_{avg}, in the same way as discussed above assuming uniform probability for all the $\binom{n_s}{4}$ different cases as follows:

$$\theta^4_{avg} = \sum_{i=1}^{\binom{n_s}{4}} \frac{\theta^4_i}{\binom{n_s}{4}} \tag{31}$$

This procedure is repeated to calculate θ^j_{avg}, $(4 < j \leq n_s)$ in the same away by adding 4 new equations for each extra docking point considered.

Finally, the average angle of rotation, θ_{avg} can be approximated as;

$$\theta_{avg} = \frac{1}{p_f} \sum_{i=3}^{n_s} p^i_f \times \theta^i_{avg} \tag{32}$$

2.4   Computing θ_{avg} Using a 3-D Coordinate System

As mentioned before, a 3-d coordinate system can be used in a similar way to compute θ_{avg}. However, as this increases the number of unknown variables appreciably, we need to assume that at least 15 docking points of the protein/ligand come within the threshold distance (to solve all the equations). This greatly increases the number of equations that has to be solved as well. Moreover, for small docking sites, the assumption of 15 docking points coming close might not be a practical way of solving the problem. Another disadvantage of the 3-d calculations is that as we need more docking points to come close, the value of θ_{avg} becomes less than what we estimate with the 2-d system, resulting in a further decrease in the estimation of the time for the rotation of the ligand axis. Fig 6 plots the rotational energy required (measured in terms of total change in free energy reported in [19]) for different number of docking points coming within threshold distance (varied from 3 to 15). The results were generated for the protein-ligand pair of human leukocyte elastase and OMTKY3 where the optimal configuration corresponds to 15 docking points coming close (as we will have maximum chance of docking in that case) and the subsequent energy requirements were assumed for lesser number of docking points coming close. We observe that as more docking points come close, the rotational energy required is lesser i.e., the ligand axis has to rotate less to reach the docked conformation

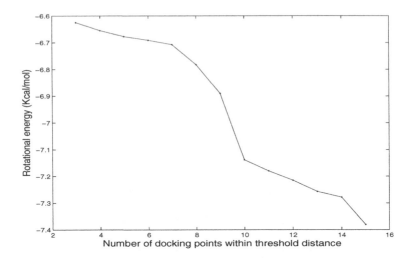

Fig. 6. Dependence of rotational energy on the number of docking points within threshold distance (the curve derived from the data points of [19])

indicating that the time required for rotation also decreases. Note that the requirements of 3 docking points coming close for the 2-d system and 15 points for the 3-d system is not specific to any protein-ligand pair and are a requirement of our model to be able to compute θ_{avg}.

As we show later, the total protein-ligand docking time is primarily governed by the collision theory component (i.e., the time required for rotation of the ligand axis is negligible in comparison to the time taken by the ligand to collide with the docking site on the protein), and hence the lesser accuracy of the 2-d based computations is not a deterrent in estimating the total docking time. Also, this reduces the number of equations that need to be solved making the model computationally fast which is a basic requirement for our discrete event-based simulator.

2.5   Calculating p_b

We assume that the ligand molecules enter the cell one at a time to initiate the binding. From the principles of collision theory for hard spheres, we model the protein and ligand molecules as rigid spheres with radii r_P and r_L respectively (Fig 7). We define our coordinate system such that the protein is stationary with respect to the ligand molecule, so that the latter moves towards the protein with a relative velocity U. The ligand molecule moves through space to sweep out a collision cross section $A = \pi r_{PL}^2$ (as illustrated in Fig 8), where r_{PL} is the collision radius given by:

$$r_{PL} = r_P + r_L$$

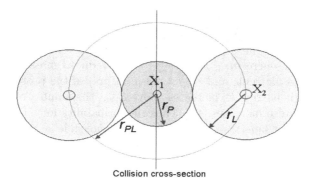

Collision cross-section

Fig. 7. Schematic diagram of protein and ligand molecules

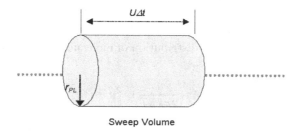

Sweep Volume

Fig. 8. Volume swept out by the ligand molecule in time Δt

The number of collisions during a time period Δt is determined when a ligand molecule will be inside the space that is created by the motion of the collision cross section over this time period due to the motion of the ligand molecule. As mentioned before, p_b denotes the probability of collision of the ligand with the protein with enough kinetic energy for the binding to occur successfully. In time Δt, the ligand molecule sweeps out a volume ΔV given by:

$$\Delta V = \pi r_{PL}^2 U \Delta t$$

Now, the probability of the ligand molecule being present in the collision volume ΔV is $p_L = 1$ (it is given that one ligand molecule arrived creating a collision volume of ΔV).

Probability of the protein being present in an arbitrary uniformly distributed ΔV in the total volume, V (V denotes the total volume of the cell), is $p_P = \Delta V.n_2/V$, where, n_2 denotes the number of protein molecules present inside the cell.

Thus, probability of the ligand molecule to collide with the protein during time Δt:

$$p_c = p_L \times p_P = \Delta V.n_2/V = \frac{n_2 \pi r_{PL}^2 U \Delta t}{V} \tag{33}$$

We next assume that the colliding ligand molecule must have free energy E_{Act} or greater to overcome the energy barrier and bind to the specific protein molecule. The kinetic energy of approach of the ligand towards the protein with a velocity U is $E = \frac{m_{PL}U^2}{2}$, where $m_{PL} = \frac{m_P \cdot m_L}{m_P + m_L}$ = the reduced mass, m_L = mass (in gm) of the ligand molecule and m_P = mass (in gm) of the protein. We assume that as the kinetic energy, E, increases above E_{Act}, the number of collisions that result in binding also increases [46]. Thus the probability for a binding to occur because of sufficient kinetic energy of the ligand molecule is given by:

$$p_r = \left\{ \begin{array}{cc} \frac{E - E_{Act}}{E}, & \text{for } E > E_{Act} \\ 0, & \text{otherwise} \end{array} \right\} \tag{34}$$

and the overall probability, p_o, for collision with sufficient energy is given by:

$$p_o = p(binding, Collision) = p_r \times p_c = \left\{ \begin{array}{cc} p_c \frac{(E - E_{Act})}{E}, & \text{for } E > E_{Act} \\ 0, & \text{otherwise.} \end{array} \right\}$$

The above equations assumed a fixed relative velocity U for the reaction. We will use the Maxwell-Boltzmann distribution of molecular velocities for a species of mass m given by:

$$f(U,T)dU = 4\pi \left(\frac{m}{2\pi k_B T}\right)^{3/2} e^{\frac{-mU^2}{2k_B T}} U^2 dU$$

where k_B = Boltzmann's constant = 1.381×10^{-23} kg $m^2/s^2/K/molecule$ and T denoting the absolute temperature. Replacing m with the reduced mass m_{PL} of the ligand and protein molecules, we get,

$$f(U,T)dU = 4\pi \left(\frac{m_{PL}}{2\pi k_B T}\right)^{3/2} e^{\frac{-m_{PL}U^2}{2k_B T}} U^2 dU \tag{35}$$

The term on the left hand side of the above equation denotes the fraction of this specific ligand molecule with relative velocities between U and $(U + dU)$. Summing up the collisions for the ligand molecule for all velocities we get the probability of collision with sufficient energy, p_b as follows:

$$p_b = \int_0^\infty p_o f(U,T)dU$$

Now, recalling $E = \frac{m_{PL}U^2}{2}$, i.e., $dE = m_{PL}U dU$ and substituting into Eqn. 35, we get:

$$f(U,T)dU = 4\pi \left(\frac{m_{PL}}{2\pi k_B T}\right)^{3/2} \frac{2E}{U m_{PL}^2} e^{\frac{-E}{k_B T}} dE$$

Thus we get:

$$\begin{aligned} p_b &= \int_{E_{Act}}^\infty \frac{(E - E_{Act})4n_2\pi r_{PL}^2 \Delta t}{V k_B T} \sqrt{\frac{1}{2\pi k_b T m_{PL}}} e^{-\frac{E}{k_b T}} dE \\ &= \frac{n_2 r_{PL}^2 \Delta t}{V} \sqrt{\frac{8\pi k_B T}{m_{PL}}} e^{\frac{-E_{Act}}{k_b T}} \end{aligned} \tag{36}$$

3   Computing the Time Taken for Protein-Ligand Docking

Now, we are in a position to analytically compute the time taken for ligand-protein docking. This can be divided into two parts: 1) computing the time taken for the ligand to collide with the binding site of the protein molecule with enough activation energy to create a temporary binding and 2) computing the time taken for the rotation of the ligand axis to stabilize the binding to the protein molecule. Note that the first part computes the time for the random collisions until the creation of the precursor state $A - B$ (as shown in Eq. 5) and involves the first two steps in Eq. 5. The second part computes the time taken for the formation of the final docked complex, AB, from $A - B$.

3.1   Time Taken for the Ligand to Collide with the Binding Site of the Protein Molecule with Enough Activation Energy for Successful Docking

Let $\Delta t = \tau =$ an infinitely small time step. The ligand molecules try to bind to the protein through collisions. If the first collision fails to produce a successful binding , they collide again after τ time units and so on.

We can interpret p_t as the probability of a successful binding in time τ. Thus, the *average time for the ligand to collide with the binding site of the protein molecule with enough activation energy for successful docking* denoted by T_1^c is given by:

$$T_1^c = p_t\tau + p_t(1 - p_t)2\tau + p_t(1 - p_t)^2 3\tau + ... = \frac{\tau}{p_t}$$

and the corresponding second moment, T_2^c, is given by:

$$T_2^c = p_t(\tau^2) + p_t(1 - p_t)(2\tau)^2 + p_t(1 - p_t)^2(3\tau)^2 + ... = \frac{(2 - p_t)\tau^2}{p_t^2}$$

The average and second moment computations follow from the concept that the successful collision can be the first collision or the second collision or the third collision and so on. We find that the time for ligand-protein collisions (which is a random variable denoted by x) follows an exponential distribution for the specific ligand and protein used to generate the results (because the mean and standard deviation are fairly equal as reported in the next section). It should be noted that as we assume τ to be quite small, we can approximate the total time measurements of binding using a continuous (exponential in this case) distribution instead of a discrete geometric distribution. Thus as reported later, we find $T_1^c \approx T_2^c$, and hence the pdf of the exponential distribution is given by:

$$f_1(x) = \left\{ \begin{array}{cc} (\frac{1}{T_1^c})e^{-(\frac{x}{T_1^c})}, & \text{for } x \geq 0 \\ 0, & \text{otherwise} \end{array} \right\} \tag{37}$$

3.2   Finding the Average Time for Rotation of Ligand Axis

Now to rotate the docking site on the ligand about the axis to reach the final docking configuration, we need to have some rotational energy which is contributed by the total change in free energy in forming the docked complex (denoted by E_f). Thus we have:

$$\frac{1}{2} I_d w_d^2 = E_f \tag{38}$$

where, I_d and w_d are respectively the average rotational inertia and angular velocity of the docking site of the ligand. Now the estimates of E_f have been reported extensively in the literature, and our goal is to calculate I_d and w_d.

Calculating the average moment of inertia of the ligand, I_d: The moment of inertia calculation can become tricky as we have to consider the axis of rotation as well as its distance from the ligand axis. Fig 9 illustrates the possible orientations of the protein and ligand axis where the dotted line with an arrow signifies the axis of rotation. Note that the protein and ligand axes might not intersect as well in some configurations (Figs 9(b),(c),(d)). In such cases, it becomes imperative to calculate the distance of the ligand axis from the point about which it rotates making the moment of inertia calculation quite cumbersome.

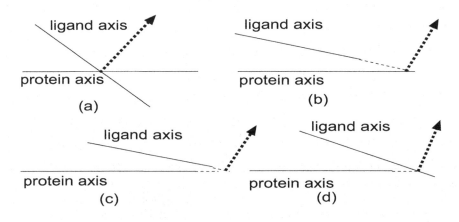

Fig. 9. Possible orientations of the protein and ligand axes

We assume that the ligand and protein axes do actually intersect in all cases (i.e. Figs 9(b),(c),(d) can never occur). This is a practical consideration because the ligand physically collides with the protein. We also assume that the ligand axis rotates about this point of intersection. Note that this simplifies the average moment of inertia calculation as the intersection point will always be on the ligand axis (and we do not have to compute the distance of the ligand axis from the axis of rotation).

From section 2.3 we can easily find the equations of the two lines denoting the protein and ligand axes (as the coordinates of at least 3 points on each line is known). Hence the point of intersection can be computed in a straightforward manner. Let the point of intersection be denoted by (δ_x, δ_y). Also, we can estimate the coordinates of the beginning (denoted by (b_x, b_y)) and end (denoted by (e_x, e_y)) points on the ligand axis corresponding to the first and last docking points 1 and n_s.

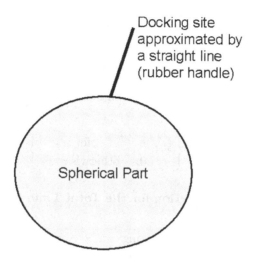

Fig. 10. Approximate model of the Ligand molecule

As explained before, the docking sites of the ligand and protein axes are assumed as straight lines, such that the ligand can be approximated as a sphere (of radius r_L) with a rubber handle (which is the straight line denoting the docking site on the ligand backbone). Fig 10 explains the model. This rubber handle on the ligand can be approximated as a cylinder with radius r_d and length $\sqrt{(b_x - e_x)^2 + (b_y - e_y)^2}$. Note that in Section 2.5 we had modelled the ligand as a hard sphere. However, the calculation of θ_{avg} and I_d requires the docking site of the ligand axis to be a straight line (for ease in computation). Note that, in general, the docking site is quite small compared to the length of the entire ligand, and thus the rubber handle assumption is quite feasible. The collision theory estimate can still treat the entire ligand as a sphere without taking into account the rubber handle part. However, because the docking site is approximated as a rubber handle, only this part rotates to bind to the corresponding site on the protein and hence I_d is the rotational inertia of the docking site only. We also assume that the docking site on the ligand has uniform density, ρ_d, and cross-sectional area, $A_d = \pi r_d^2$. Thus we can approximate I_d as follows:

$$I_d = \int_{-\sqrt{(\delta_x - e_x)^2 + (\delta_y - e_y)^2}}^{\sqrt{(\delta_x - b_x)^2 + (\delta_y - b_y)^2}} \rho_d A_d x^2 \, dx$$

$$= \frac{\rho_d A_d}{3} ([(\delta_x - e_x)^2 + (\delta_y - e_y)^2]^{\frac{3}{2}} + [(\delta_x - b_x)^2 + (\delta_y - b_y)^2]^{\frac{3}{2}}) \qquad (39)$$

Calculating T_1^r: The average time for rotation of the docking site of the ligand axis (denoted by T_1^r) is given by:

$$T_1^r = \frac{\theta_{avg}}{w_d} \qquad (40)$$

However, this does not allow us to compute the second moment of the time for rotation. We assume that the time for rotation follows an exponential distribution and hence the second moment of the time for rotation is given by:

$$T_2^r = 2(T_1^r)^2 \qquad (41)$$

Thus this exponential distribution has both mean and standard deviation as T_1^r and pdf of the form:

$$f_2(x) = \left\{ \begin{array}{c} (\frac{1}{T_1^r})e^{-(\frac{x}{T_1^r})}, \quad \text{for } x \geq 0 \\ 0, \quad \text{otherwise} \end{array} \right\} \qquad (42)$$

3.3 The General Distribution for the Total Time for Protein-Ligand Docking

The total time for protein-ligand docking can be computed from the convolution of the two pdf's given in Eqns 37 and 42 as follows:

$$f(x) = f_1(x) \bigodot f_2(x) = \int_0^x f_1(z) f_2(x - z) \, dz$$

where, $f(x)$ denotes the pdf of the general distribution for the total time and $\bigodot$ is the convolution operator. Hence we get:

$$f(x) = \left\{ \begin{array}{c} \frac{e^{-\frac{x}{T_1^c}} - e^{-\frac{x}{T_1^r}}}{T_1^c - T_1^r}, \quad \text{for } x \geq 0 \\ 0, \quad \text{otherwise} \end{array} \right\} \qquad (43)$$

Also we have:

$$T_1 = \int_0^\infty x f(x) \, dx = T_1^c + T_1^r; \quad T_2 = \int_0^\infty x^2 f(x) \, dx = 2[(T_1^c)^2 + T_1^c T_1^r + (T_1^r)^2]$$

where, T_1 and T_2 are the first and second moments of the total time taken for protein-ligand docking.

4   Results and Analysis

4.1   Problems in Validation of Our Model

Before presenting the results, we first discuss the difficulty of experimentally validating our model. Note that we compute the average time for protein-ligand binding in this paper. Existing experimental results are based on estimation of the binding rate of the ligands to a specific protein. We consider the binding of the turkey ovomucoid third domain (OMTKY) ligand to the human leukocyte elastase protein to generate the results. The experimental rate constant of $10^6 M^{-1} s^{-1}$ as reported in [19] is derived from these rate measurements. Hence, the number of ligands in the cell will affect this estimate of time taken by one single ligand to bind to the protein because the rate of reaction incorporates the ligand concentration as well. However, our model computes the time taken by *any particular* ligand to bind to the protein which should be independent of the number of ligands in the cell. It is currently very difficult to carry out experiments to track a particular ligand and physically compute the time. Also, the stochastic nature of the binding process suggests that the distribution of the time taken will have a very high variance. In other words, in some cases the ligand requires time in microseconds whereas in other cases it might take as long as 1 second. The results (for the ligand-protein pair identified above) we present in the next section assume that the time taken for any particular OMTKY-human leukocyte elastase binding has a rate constant of $10^6 M^{-1} s^{-1}$ (as reported in [19]) even though it cannot be a true estimate of this event. Also, note that our model can be easily extended to incorporate the effects of multiple ligands present in the cell on the binding rate as discussed in Section 5.2.

4.2 Numerical Results

In this section, we present the numerical results for the theoretical model derived in the paper. Figs 11-15 present the results for OMTKY-Human leukocyte elastase binding in an average human cell with 20 μm diameter. Also, the results were generated for $n_s = 8$ docking points on the protein/ligand. The different parameters assumed for the numerical results are concisely presented in Table 1. We used actual values from the from the PDB database [7] and some assumptions as reported in [19].

Calculation of I_d and w_d. To calculate I_d we need to know the point of intersection of the straight lines denoting the docking sites of the protein and ligand. Because, we need to estimate the average rotational inertia, we consider two cases: (1) the intersecting point is at the center of the docking site on the ligand and (2) the intersecting point is at the end of the docking site on the ligand. Note that the coordinates of the exact set of docking points and their corresponding points on the protein/ligand backbones have been estimated using the LPC software [24]. Also the density of the ligand molecule is assumed to be 1.44 g/cm^3 as the molecular weight of OMTKY is $\approx$ 6 KDalton (see [23] for details).

The corresponding values for w_d (assuming $E_f = -7$ Kcal/mol, from [19]) are 63.5×10^9 and 31.75×10^9 radians/sec respectively. Note that, [25] reports that the average angular velocity of a protein molecule is in the range $\approx 10^9$ radians/sec, which is very close to our estimate.

Table 1. Parameter Estimation for an average Human Cell

Parameters	Eukaryotic Cell
V	$4.187 \times 10^{-15} m^3$ (average volume of a human cell)
r_P	23.24×10^{-10} m (for *Human leukocyte elastase*)
r_L	14.15×10^{-10} m (for *Turkey ovomucoid third domain*)
n_s	8
r_d	1 nm
E_f (total change in free energy)	-7 Kcal/mol [19]
m_P	23328.2 Dalton (for *Human leukocyte elastase*)
Number of ligand (OMTKY) molecules	10^5
m_L	6047.9 Dalton (for *Turkey ovomucoid third domain*)
ρ_d	1.44 g/cm^3 (for *Turkey ovomucoid third domain* [23])

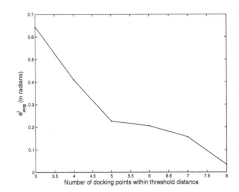

Fig. 11. θ^i_{avg} against number of docking points within threshold distance

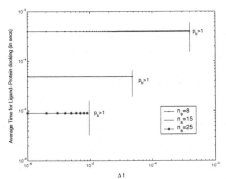

Fig. 12. Average Time against Δt for different n_s

Estimation of θ_{avg}. Fig 11 plots θ^i_{avg}, $(3 \leq i \leq 8)$, against the number of docking points coming within threshold distance of $\gamma = 2 \times 10^{-10}$ m. Note that instead of averaging out the $\binom{n_s}{i}$ possible cases of choosing i docking points, we assumed that only i contiguous points can come within a distance of γ. This is because, for the other combinations, the angle was too small making the corresponding θ^i_{avg} too low. Thus, Eq 26 was modified as follows to generate the results:

$$\theta^i_{avg} = \sum_{j=1}^{n_s-i+1} \frac{\theta^i_j}{n_s - i + 1} \qquad (44)$$

As expected, we find that the angle reduces as more docking points come within threshold distance. Also, we calculate $\theta_{avg} = 0.643483$ radians for the specific ligand-protein pair under consideration.

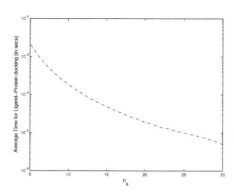
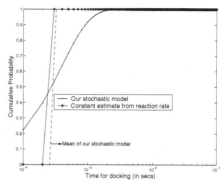

Fig. 13. Average Time against n_s

Fig. 14. Cumulative probability distribution for the ligand-protein docking time

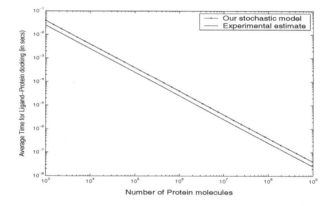

Fig. 15. Average Time against number of Protein molecules (n_2).

Estimation of T_1^r. The next step is to estimate the mean of the time for rotation of the docking site of the ligand axis to produce the final docked complex. We obviously get $T_1^r \approx 1 \times 10^{-11}$ and 2×10^{-11} secs for the two w_d estimates reported previously. Thus in general we can say that the time for rotation is too small in comparison to the time for collision, T_1^c as reported subsequently. Thus the total time for ligand-protein docking is dominated by T_1^c which corroborates the results reported in [19].

Dependence of T_1 on Δt. Fig 12 plots T_1 against different values for Δt. The average time for ligand-protein docking remains constant with increasing Δt. The same characteristics are seen for different number of docking points considered, $n_s = 8, 15, 25$ respectively. Though we have $n_s = 8$ for the ligand-protein pair under consideration, we have reported the plots for different values of n_s to show the dependence of the average binding time on n_s. The activation energy, E_{act} is kept at 0 for the above plots. For, $n_s = 8$, we find $T_1 = 0.000395$ secs as against 0.00025 secs as estimated from the experimental rate constant value of $10^6 M^{-1} s^{-1}$. This is a very important finding from our model. It states that for the process of ligand-protein docking no activation energy is required, i.e. the ligand molecules do not have to overcome an energy barrier for successful docking. Indeed, biological experiments have indicated that the docking process occurs due to changes in monomer bonds into dimers and the resultant change in free energy is used for the rotational motion of the ligand to achieve the final docked conformation. Thus this finding corroborates the validity of our model. The results were generated assuming an average of 10^5 molecules of OMTKY inside the cell.

Also it can be noted that the average time for binding (= 0.000395 secs) is very high compared to our estimate of T_1^r. Thus it can be inferred that the time taken for the rotational motion of the ligand is negligible in comparison to T_1^c.

It is to be noted that p_b as calculated above also corresponds to the number of collisions in time Δt of the ligand molecule with the protein. And for our assumption of at most one collision taking place in Δt to hold, we have to make sure that $0 \leq p_b \leq 1$ (this is also true because p_b is a probability). Thus the *regions to the right of the vertical lines* corresponding to each n_s plot denotes the forbidden region where $p_b > 1$ even though $0 \leq p \leq 1$. This gives us an estimate of the allowable Δt values for different n_s's such that T_1 indeed remains constant. Out estimates show that with $\Delta t \leq 10^{-8}$, T_1 remains constant for most values of n_s.

Dependence of T_1 on n_s. Fig 13 plots T_1 against the different possible n_s values and we find that the average time for docking decreases as the total number of docking points n_s is increased. This is again logical as the ligand molecules now have more options for binding resulting in a higher value of p_f and subsequently p_t.

The stochastic nature of the docking time. Fig 14 plots the cumulative distribution function (CDF) for the total time of binding with $E_{act} = 0$. The time for collision followed an *exponential distribution* (as the calculated mean was very close to the standard deviation). Also, because the T_1^r component is very small in comparison to T_1^c, the overall time for binding can be approximated to follow an exponential distribution given by Eq 37. Note that incorporating $T_1^r \ll T_1^c$ in Eq 43 we get Eq 37 implying that the total time for docking is dominated by the exponential distribution outlined in Eq 37.

Fig 15 illustrates the dependence of the average time for docking (T_1) on the number of protein (Human Leukocyte elastase) molecules in the cell for a fixed number of ligand (OMTKY) molecules ($\approx 10^5$). The corresponding time of reactions estimated from the experimental rate constant of $10^6 M^{-1} s^{-1}$ have also been reported. The docking time estimates from our theoretical model very closely matches the experimental estimates in the acceptable range of the number of protein molecules (varied from $10^3 - 10^9$ molecules as can be found in any standard human cell).

4.3 Important Observations

1. Our model achieves the experimental rate constant estimate with *zero* activation energy requirement for the protein-ligand pair under consideration in human cells. The stochastic nature of protein-ligand binding time can be approximated by a general distribution with pdf of the form given in Eq 43 and first and second moments given by T_1 and T_2 respectively. However, for this protein-ligand pair, the total docking time can be approximated as an exponential distribution with pdf given by Eq 37 as $T_1^r \ll T_1^c$.
2. The average time for DNA-protein binding is independent of Δt and decreases as the length of the docking site increases (i.e., as n_s increases).
3. An acceptable estimate of Δt is 10^{-8} secs. Fig 12 shows the dependence of the average time on Δt. We find that a wider range of Δt is available (keeping $p_b \leq 1$) as n_s decreases.
4. The mean of the total docking time (T_1) decreases as the length of the docking site (n_s) increases.
5. The average angle of rotation (θ) for the ligand to reach the final docked conformation is very small. This coupled with the fact that the average angular velocity of the docking site on the ligand axis being very high makes the mean time taken for rotation negligible in comparison to the collision theory component of the docking time.

5 Discussion

5.1 Limitations of Our Model

Maxwell-Boltzman distribution of molecular velocities. The Maxwell-Boltzmann distribution gives a good estimate of molecular velocities and is widely used in practice. Molecular dynamic (MD) simulation measurements during protein reactions show that the velocity distribution of proteins in the cytoplasm closely match the Maxwell-Boltzmann distribution. However, its application in our collision theory model might not give perfect results. Ideally the velocity distribution should incorporate the properties of the cytoplasm, the protein/ligand structure and also the electrostatic forces that come into play. We plan to extend our model to incorporate more realistic velocity distributions in the future.

3-D protein/ligand structure. Another point to note is that the p_f estimation can be improved by considering the 3-D structures of the protein and the ligand. Ideally, the motifs of the protein/ligand molecules are located towards the outer surface such that our straight line assumption of the docking sites are quite realistic. However, the denominator in the expression for p_f^i considers all possible atoms on the protein/ligand molecules. However, due to their 3-d structure, not all of these molecules are exposed towards the outer protein surface that the ligand can collide to. As a result our estimates of p_f^i is actually a little lower than what should be a good estimate for the same, resulting in a corresponding decrease in p_f and hence p_t and a resultant increase in T_1^c and hence T_1. This might as well explain the slightly greater time reported from our model in comparison to the experimental estimates (recall that the experimental estimate was 0.00025 secs as against the 0.000395 secs reported by our model).

Straight line assumption of the docking sites on the protein/ligand backbones. As mentioned before, we have approximated the docking site on the protein/ligand axes as straight lines to simplify the computations of the average angle of rotation θ_{avg} and subsequently the average time required for rotation, T_1^r. However, because $T_1^r \ll T_1^c$, the T_1^r component of T_1 is negligible and the results reported from our theoretical model are quite close to experimental estimates. We are working on this aspect to identify a better estimate of T_1^r that models the actual docking process more closely.

5.2   Biological Implications

Several ligands coming into the cell for docking. If we consider several ligands searching for their docking sites on the protein simultaneously, our results still remain valid. Note that as the number of ligands increase in the cell, the binding rate will increase. Assuming the docking time to be completely characterized by the collision theory part, an analytical estimate of the binding rate in such cases can be achieved by using the batch model of [11]. However, the time taken for any particular ligand to bind to the corresponding protein molecule still remains the same. Thus increasing the number of ligands should not change the results that we report for any particular ligand. In fact, this discrepancy arises because of the definition of the binding rate the inverse of which gives the time required for a successful docking to occur between the protein-ligand pair. Looking into the problem from one specific ligand's perspective (as we do in this paper), the average time required for docking will be the same assuming there are enough number of protein molecules in the cell. This is a salient feature of our stochastic simulation paradigm where we track the course of events initiated by any particular molecule in the cell to study the dynamics of the entire cell. However, this may cause molecular crowding (of ligands) in the cell which can have an impact on the search time. Further studies are required to cover this aspect of ligand-protein docking.

Funnels and local organization of sites. Local arrangement of the binding sites of proteins tend to create a funnel in the binding energy landscape leading to more rapid binding of cognate sites. Our model assumes no such funnels of energy field. If the ligands spend most of their search time far from the cognate site our model will remain valid and no significant decrease in binding time is expected.

6   Conclusion

We have presented a computationally simplified model to estimate the ligand-protein binding time based on collision theory. The motivation for this simplified model is to construct a simulation that can model a complex biological system which is currently beyond the scope of kinetic rate based simulations. The model is robust enough as the major contributing factors (molecular motion) are captured in a reasonably accurate way for general cell environments. For an extreme cell environment condition, where the influence of the electrostatic force will be significantly different, the model will not provide such accuracy. We are exploring the possibility to modify the velocity distribution to capture the effect of this extreme cell environment. However, the model is computationally fast and allows our stochastic simulator to model complex biological systems at the molecular level (i.e., that involves many such docking events). The proposed mechanism is not only limited to protein-ligand interactions but provide a general framework for protein-DNA binding. The complexity of the 3-d protein/ligand structures have been simplified in this paper to achieve acceptable estimates of the holding time of the ligand-protein binding event. We found that no activation energy is required for the docking process and the rotational energy for ligand-protein complex to attain the final docked conformation is contributed by the total change in free energy of the complex. The proposed mechanism has important biological implications in explaining how a ligand can find its docking site on the protein, in vivo, in the presence of other proteins and by a simultaneous search of several ligands. Besides providing a quantitative framework for analysis of the kinetics of ligand-protein binding, our model also links molecular properties of the ligand/protein and the structure of the docking sites on the ligand/protein backbones to the timing of the docking event. This provides us with a general parametric model for this biological function for our discrete-event based simulation framework. Once the model is validated for a few test cases, it can serve as a parametric model that can be used for all ligand-protein binding scenarios where the binding details are available. This may eliminate the necessity of conducting specific experiments for determining the rate constants to model a complex biological process.

References

1. Human Genome Project,
   http://www.ornl.gov/sci/techresources/Human_Genome/home.shtml
2. Schena, M.: Microarray Analysis, ISBN: 0471414433 (2002)
3. Duggan, D.J., Bittner, M., Chen, Y., Meltzer, P., Trent, J.M.: Expression profiling using cDNA microarrays. Nature Genetics Supplement 21, 10–14 (1999)
4. McCulloch, A.D., Huber, G.: Integrative biological modeling in silico. In Silico Simulation of Biological Processes, Novartis Foundation Symposium 247 (2002)
5. Bower, J.A., Bolouri, H.: Computational Modeling of Genetic and Biological Network. MIT Press, Cambridge (2001)
6. Hunter, P., Nielsen, P., Bullivant, D.: In Silico Simulation of Biological Processes. In: Novartis Foundation Symposium No. 247, pp. 207–221. Wiley, Chichester (2002)

7. The RCSB Protein Data Bank, http://www.rcsb.org/pdb/
8. von Hippel, P.H., Berg, O.G.: On the specificity of DNA-protein interactions. In: Proc. Natl. Acad. Sci., USA, vol. 83, pp. 1608–1612 (1986)
9. Ghosh, S., Ghosh, P., Basu, K., Das, S., Daefler, S.: SimBioSys: A Discrete Event Simulation Platform for 'in silico' Study of Biological Systems. In: Proceedings of 39th IEEE Annual Simulation Symposium, Huntsville, AL (April 2 - 6, 2006)
10. Ghosh, P., Ghosh, S., Basu, K., Das, S., Daefler, S.: An Analytical Model to Estimate the time taken for Cytoplasmic Reactions for Stochastic Simulation of Complex Biological Systems. In: 2nd IEEE Granular Computing Conf., USA (2006)
11. Ghosh, P., Ghosh, S., Basu, K., Das, S., Daefler, S.: Stochastoc Modeling of Cytoplasmic Reactions for Complex Biological Systems. In: IEE International Conference on Computational Science and its Applications, Glasgow, Scotland, May 8-11 (2006)
12. Ghosh, S., Ghosh, P., Basu, K., Das, S.K.: iSimBioSys: An 'In Silico' Discrete Event Simulation Framework for Modeling Biological Systems. IEEE Comp. Systems BioInf. Conf. (2005)
13. Hasty, J., Collins, J.J.: Translating the Noise. Nature 31, 13–14 (2002)
14. Gillespie, D.T.: Exact stochastic simulation of coupled chemical reactions. J. Phys. Chem. 81(25), 2340–2361 (1977)
15. Kitano, H.: Cell Designer: A modeling tool of biochemical networks. online at, http://www.celldesigner.org/
16. Adalsteinsson, D., McMillen, D., Elston, T.C.: Biochemical Network Stochastic Simulator (BioNets): software for stochastic modeling of biochemical networks. BMC Bioinformatics (March 2004)
17. Le Novre, N., Shimizu, T.S.: StochSim: modeling of stochastic biomolecular processes. Bioinformatics 17, 575–576 (2000)
18. Cell Illustrator. online at, http://www.fqspl.com.pl/
19. Camacho, C.J., Kimura, S.R., DeLisi, C., Vajda, S.: Kinetics of Desolvation-Mediated Protein-Protein Binding. Biophysical Journal 78, 1094–1105 (2000)
20. DeLisi, C., Wiegel, F.: Effect of nonspecific forces and finite receptor number on rate constants of ligand-cell-bound-receptor interactions. In: Proc. Natl. Acad. Sci., 78th edn., USA, pp. 5569–5572 (1981)
21. Smoluchowski, M.V.: Versuch einer mathematischen Theorie der Koagulationskinetik kolloider Loeschungen. Z. Phys. Chem. 92, 129–168
22. Northrup, S.H., Erickson, H.P.: Kinetics of proteinprotein association explained by Brownian dynamics computer simulations. In: Proc. Natl. Acad. Sci., USA, vol. 89, pp. 3338–3342 (1992)
23. Fischer, H., Polikarpov, I., Craievich, A.F.: Average protein density is a molecular-weight-dependent function. Protein Science 13, 2825–2828 (2004)
24. Sobolev, V., Sorokine, A., Prilusky, J., Abola, E.E., Edelman, M.: Automated analysis of interatomic contacts in proteins. Bioinformatics 15, 327–332 (1999)
25. Nanomedicine, vol. I: Basic Capabilities, http://www.nanomedicine.com/NMI/3.2.5.htm
26. Camacho, C., Weng, Z., Vajda, S., De Lisi, C.: Biophisics J, vol. 76, pp. 1166–1178 (1999)
27. Camacho, C., De Lisi, C., Vajda, S.: Thermodynamics of the Drug-Receptor Interactions. In: Raffa, R. (ed.) Wiley, London (2001)
28. Camacho, C., Vajda, S.: Protein docking along smooth association pathways. PNAS 98(19), 10636–10641 (2001)
29. Sharp, K., Fine, R., Honig, B.: Computer simulations of the diffusion of a substrate to an active site of an enzyme. Science 236, 1460–1463 (1987)

30. Stone, R., Dennis, S., Hofsteenge, J.: Quantitative evaluation of the contribution of ionic interactions to the formation of thrombin-hirudin complex. Biochemistry 28, 6857–6863 (1989)
31. Eltis, L., Herbert, R., Barker, P., Mauk, A., Northrup, S.: Reduction of horse ferricytochrome c by bovine liver ferrocytochrome b_5. Experimental and theoretical analysis. Biochemistry 30, 3663–3674 (1991)
32. Schreiber, G., Fersht, A.: Rapid, electrostatically assisted association of proteins. Nature Struct. Biol. 3, 427–431 (1996)
33. Gabdoulline, R., Wade, R.: Simulation of the diffusional association of barnase and barstar. Biophisics J. 72, 1917–1929 (1997)
34. Vijaykumar, M., Wong, K., Schreiber, G., Fersht, A., Szabo, A., Zhou, H.: Electrostatic enhancement of diffusion-controlled protein-protein association: comparison of theory and experiment on Barnase and Barstar. J. Mol. Biol. 278, 1015–1024 (1998)
35. Chothia, C., Janin, J.: Principles of protein-protein recognition. Nature 256, 705–708 (1975)
36. Camacho, C., Weng, Z., Vajda, S., DeLisi, C.: Free energy landscapes of encounter complexes in protein-protein association. Biophisics J. 76, 1166–1178 (1999)
37. Tomita, M., et al.: ECell: Software environment for whole cell simulation. Bioinformatics 15(1), 72–84 (1999)
38. Sauro, H.M.: Jarnac: a system for interactive metabolic analysis. Animating the Cellular Map. In: 9th International BioThermoKinetics Meeting, Stellenbosch University Press, ch. 33, pp. 221–228 (2000)
39. Ghosh, P., Ghosh, S., Basu, K., Das, S., Daefler, S.: Modeling the Diffusion process in Stochastic Event based Simulation of the PhoPQ system. International Symposium on Computational Biology and Bioinformatics (ISBB), India (December 2006)
40. Ghosh, P., Ghosh, S., Basu, K., Das, S.K.: Modeling protein-DNA binding time in Stochastic Discrete Event Simulation of Biological Processes. submitted to the Recomb Satellite Conference on Systems Biology, San Diego, USA (November 2006)
41. Regev, A., Silverman, W., Shapiro, E.: Representation and simulation of biochemical processes using the π-calculus process algebra. In: Proceedings of the Pacific Symposium of Biocomputing 2001 (PSB2001), vol. 6, pp. 459–470
42. Priami, C., Regev, A., Silverman, W., Shapiro, E.: Application of a stochastic name passing calculus to representation and simulation of molecular processes. Information Processing Letters 80, 25–31
43. Regev, A.: Representation and simulation of molecular pathways in the stochastic π-calculus. In: Proceedings of the 2nd workshop on Computation of Biochemical Pathways and Genetic Networks (2001)
44. Regev, A., Silverman, W., Shapiro, E.: Representing biomolecular processes with computer process algebra: π-calculus programs of signal transduction pathways. In: Proceedings of the Pacific Symposium of Biocomputing 2000, World Scientific Press, Singapore
45. Finn, R.D., Marshall, M., Bateman, A.: iPfam: visualization of protein-protein interactions in PDB at domain and amino acid resolutions. Bioinformatics 21, 410–412 (2005)
46. Fogler, H., Gurmen, M.: Elements of Chemical Reaction Engineering. ch. 3.1, online at http://www.engin.umich.edu/cre/03chap/html/collision/

Equation-Based Congestion Control in the Internet Biologic Environment

Morteza Analoui and Shahram Jamali

IUST University, Narmak, Tehran, Iran
{analoui, jamali}@iust.ac.ir

Abstract. In this paper we present a new aspect of human kind life that is the Internet. We call this new ecosystem IBE (Internet Biologic Environment). As a first step in modeling of IBE we view it from point of congestion control and develop an algorithm that utilizes some aspects of biologically inspired mathematical models as a nontraditional approach to design of congestion control in communication networks. We show that the interaction of those Internet entities that involved in congestion control mechanisms is similar to predator-prey and competition interactions. We combine the mathematical models of predator-prey and competition interactions to obtain a hybrid model and apply it in congestion control issue. Simulation results show that using appropriately defined parameters, this model leads to a stable, fair and high-performance congestion control algorithm.

Keywords: Communication Networks, Congestion Control, Bio-Inspired Computing, Competition and Predator-Prey.

1 Introduction

The human kind is confronting a new biological life, which is the Internet. The Internet as a new environment has a variety of species. Internet species include the human, applications, software, computers, protocols, algorithms and so on. The interactions of these species determine the dynamics of this ecology. We believe that the consideration of the Internet as a biologic environment can originate two areas of benefits:

Bio-Inspired Network Control

Technology is taking us to a world where myriads of heavily networked devices interact with the physical world in multiple ways, and at multiple scales, from the global Internet scale down to micro- and nano-devices. A fundamental research challenge is the design of robust decentralized computing systems capable of operating under changing environments and noisy input, and yet exhibits the desired behavior and response time. These systems should be able to adapt and learn how to react to unforeseen scenarios as well as to display properties comparable to social entities. Biological systems are able to handle many of these challenges with an

C. Priami (Ed.): Trans. on Comput. Syst. Biol. VIII, LNBI 4780, pp. 42–62, 2007.

elegance and efficiency still far beyond current human artifacts. Based on this observation, bio-inspired approaches have been proposed in the past years as a strategy to handle the complexity of such systems.

Network-Based Biology Analysis, Design and Control

Network analysis and modeling address a wide spectrum of techniques for studying artificial and natural networks. It refers domains consisting of individuals that are linked together into complex networks, communication networks, social networks and biological networks. They constitute a very active area of research in a variety of scientific disciplines, including communication, Biology, Artificial Intelligence and Mathematics. More recently, the study of communication networks has gained increased attention in modeling diverse areas of Internet, such as performance, security, congestion control, and so on. We believe that the techniques developed for the analysis of Internet can provide a substantial background for studying the structure, dynamics and evolution of complex biological networks. Hence, the biologists can borrow this background to study aspects such as population dynamics, fault tolerance, adaptability, complexity, information flow, community structures, and propagation patterns.

In order to study and analysis Internet Biologic Environment (IBE), we need to model it. The following models can be proposed for IBE: Performance Model, Management Model, Security Model, Congestion Control Model and so on. In this paper we are going to model this new biological life of the human kind. As the first step the congestion control modeling is considered. The central aim of this paper is to obtain bio-inspired methods to engineer congestion control.

Previous Internet research has been heavily based on measurements and simulations, which have intrinsic limitations. For example, network measurements cannot tell us the effects of new protocols before their deployment. Simulations only work for small networks with simple topology due to the constraints of the memory size and processor speed. We cannot assume that a protocol that works in a small network will still perform well in the Internet [4]. A theoretical framework and especially mathematical models can greatly help us understand the advantages and shortcomings of current Internet technologies and guide us to design new protocols for identified problems and future networks. The steady-state throughput of TCP Reno has been studied based on the stationary distribution of congestion windows, e.g. [5, 6, 7, 8]. These studies show that the TCP throughput is inversely proportional to end-to-end delay and to the square root of packet loss probability. Padhye [9] refined the model to capture the fast retransmit mechanism and the time-out effect, and achieved a more accurate formula. This equilibrium property of TCP Reno is used to define the notion of TCP–friendliness and motivates the equation based congestion control [10]. Misra [11, 12] proposed an ordinary differential equation model of the dynamics of TCP Reno, which is derived by studying congestion window size with a stochastic differential equation. This deterministic model treats the rate as fluid quantities (by assuming that the packet is infinitely small) and ignores the randomness in packet level, in contrast to the classical queuing theory approach, which relies on stochastic models. This model has been quickly combined with feedback control theory to study the dynamics of TCP systems, e.g. [13, 14], and to design stable AQM (Active Queue Management) algorithms, e.g. [15, 16, 17, 18, 19]. Similar flow models for other TCP schemes are also developed, e.g. [20, 21] for TCP Vegas, and [22, 23] for FAST TCP. The analysis and design of protocols for large-scale network have been made possible with the optimization framework and the duality model. Kelly [24, 25] formulated the bandwidth allocation problem as a utility maximization over source rates with capacity constraints. A distributed algorithm is also provided by Kelly [25] to globally solve the penalty function form of this optimization problem. This algorithm is called the primal algorithm where the sources adapt their rates dynamically, and the link prices are calculated by a static function of arrival rates. Low and Lapsley [26] proposed a gradient projection algorithm to solve its dual problem. It is shown that this algorithm globally converges to the exact solution of the original optimization problem since there is no duality gap. This approach is called the dual algorithm, where links adapt their prices dynamically, and the users' source rates are determined by a static function.

In the current paper, we use some well-established biological mathematical models, and apply them to congestion control scheme of communication networks to gain a bio-inspired equation-based congestion control algorithm.

In section 2, we present a conceptual framework for Biologically Inspired network Control (BICC) and a literature about the models of interacting populations and explain analogy between the biological interaction and the communication networks. Section 3 presents a case study and introduces a methodology for applying the predator-prey to the Internet congestion control scheme. It gives an example and discusses the stability, the fairness and the performance of the introduced solution for its congestion control algorithm. In Section 4 we present another case study for applying the combinational model of competition and predator-prey models to the Internet congestion control scheme. The implementation consideration for the proposed algorithms will be given in section 5. In section 6 we talk about "how the system biology benefits from this work". We conclude in section 7 with future works.

2   A Conceptual Framework: Internet as an Ecosystem Analogy

The first step in bio-inspired computation should be to develop more sophisticated biological models as sources of computational inspiration, and to use a conceptual framework to develop and analyze the computational metaphors and algorithms. We believe that bio-inspired algorithms are best developed and analyzed in the context of a multidisciplinary conceptual framework that provides for sophisticated biological models and well-founded analytical principles. In the reverse direction, the techniques, algorithms, protocols and analytical models, etc. that are developed for analysis of Internet, provide a significant background for research in bionetwork area.

Fig. 1 illustrates a possible structure for such a conceptual framework. Here probes (observations and experiments) are used to provide a (partial and noisy) view of the complex biological system. From this limited view, we build and validate simplifying abstract representations and models of the biology. From these biological models, we build and validate analytical computational frameworks. Validation may use mathematical analysis, benchmark problems, and engineering demonstrators. These frameworks provide principles for designing and analyzing bio-inspired algorithms

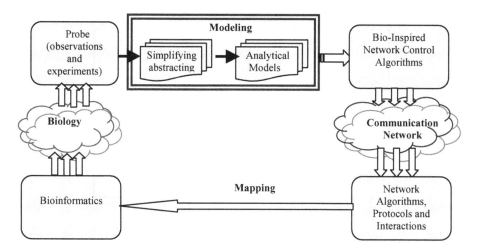

Fig. 1. An outline conceptual framework for a bio-inspired computational domain

applicable to non-biological problems, possibly tailored to a range of problem domains and contain as much or as little biological realism as appropriate. The concept flow also supports the design of algorithms specifically tailored to modeling the original biological domain, permits influencing and validating the structure of the biological models, and can help suggest ideas of further experiments to probe the biological system. This is necessarily an interdisciplinary process, requiring collaboration between (at least) biologists, mathematicians, and computer scientists to build a complete framework.

2.1   Internet Ecology

Consider a network with a set of k source nodes and a set of k destination nodes. We denote $S=\{S_1, S_2, ..., S_k\}$ as the set of source nodes with identical round-trip propagation delay (RTT), and $D=\{D_1, D_2, ..., D_k\}$ as the set of destination nodes. Our network model consists of a bottleneck link from LAN to WAN as shown in Fig. 2 and uses a window-based algorithm for congestion control. The bottleneck link has capacity of B packet per RRT. The congestion window (W) is a sender-side limit on

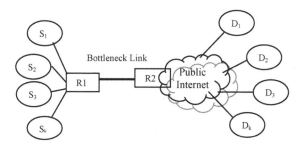

Fig. 2. General Network Model

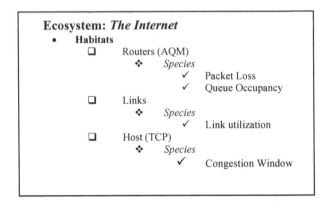

Fig. 3. Internet Ecosystem Typology

the amount of data the sender can transmit into the network before receiving an acknowledgment (*ACK*). We assume that all connections are long-lived and have unlimited bulk data for communication.

In analogy, this network can be viewed as an ecosystem that connects a wide variety of habitats such as routers, hosts, links and operating systems (OS), and etc. We consider that there is some species in these habitats such as *"Human"*, *"Computers"*, *"Congestion Window"*(W), *"Packet Drop"*(P) and *"Queue Length"*(q), *"link utilization" (u) and so on.* Fig. 3 shows the typology of Internet ecosystem from congestion control perspective. Since these species interact, the population size of each species is affected. In general, there is a whole web of interacting species, which makes for structurally complex communities. Fig. 3 shows that the Congestion Window (W) is a species that lives in the hosts. Let the population of W in source Si be W_i *(congestion window size of connection i)* and assume that each organism of this population sends one packet in each *RTT*. It is clear that if the population of this species is increased, then the number of sent packet will be inflated; hence, the population size of W should be controlled to avoid congestion. In order to control the population size of W species, we use some population control tactics of nature. In the following sections, we propose a methodology to use "Perdition" and "Competition" tactics for this purpose.

2.2 Types of Population Interactions

As mentioned, we need to build and validate simplifying abstract representations and models of the biology. Since the population control tactics of nature are candidate to be used for bio-inspired congestion control algorithms, hence, let us take an overview of types of population interactions, to put the rest of this section in context [27]. These interactions can be considered between populations:

Mutualism: Mutualism is any relationship between two species of organisms that benefits both species. Most people think of when they use the word "symbiosis" this relationship.

Herbivores: Herbivores eats pieces of plants, this harms the plant in some way, and population growth is slowed.

Parasites: Parasites do not kill the host outright, necessarily. They might cause it to be weak and die for other reasons, or might make lower the birth rate.

Predation: This interaction refers to classical predators that kill individuals and eat them; such as carnivores, insectivores and etc. We can summarize this interaction as below:

(**1**) In the absence of predators, prey would grow exponentially. (**2**) The effect of predation is to reduce the prey's growth rate. (**3**) In the absence of prey, predators will decline exponentially. (**4**) The prey's contribution to the predator's growth rate is proportional to the available prey as well as to the size of the predator population. There are no handling time or satiation constraints on predators.

One of the first models to incorporate interactions between predators and prey was proposed in 1925 by the American biophysicist Alfred Lotka and the Italian mathematician Vito Volterra. The Lotka-Volterra model [28] describes interactions between two species in an ecosystem, a predator and a prey. Since we are considering two species, the model will involve two equations, one, which describes how the prey population changes, and the second, which describes how the predator population changes. For concreteness, let us assume that the preys in our model are rabbits, and that the predators are foxes. If we let $r(t)$ and $f(t)$ represent the number of rabbits and foxes, respectively, that are alive at time t, then the Lotka-Volterra model is:

$$\begin{cases} \dfrac{dr}{dt} = ar - brf & (1) \\ \dfrac{df}{dt} = crf - df & (2) \end{cases}$$

Where the parameters are defined by:

a is the natural growth rate of rabbits in the absence of predation, b is the death rate per encounter of rabbits due to predation, c is the efficiency of turning predated rabbits into foxes, d is the natural death rate of foxes in the absence of food (rabbits).

For example there is a classical set of data on a pair of interacting populations that come close: the **Canadian lynx** and **snowshoe hare** pelt-trading records of the Hudson Bay Company over almost a century. Fig. 4 (from Odum, *Fundamentals of Ecology*, Saunders, 1953) shows a plot of that data.

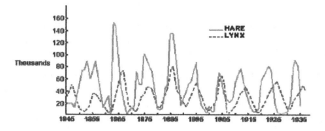

Fig. 4. Fluctuation in the number of pelts

Competition: Here two or more species compete for the same limited food source or in some way inhibit each other's growth. For example, competition may be for territory, which is directly related to food resources. Here we discuss a very simple competition model, which demonstrates a general principle, which is observed to hold in Nature, namely, that when two species compete for the same limited resources. Consider the basic 2-species Lotka–Volterra competition model with each species n_1 and n_2 having logistic growth in the absence of the other. Inclusion of logistic growth in the Lotka–Volterra systems makes them much more realistic, but to highlight the principle we consider the simpler model which nevertheless reflects many of the properties of more complicated models, particularly as regards stability. We thus consider.

$$\frac{dn_1}{dt} = h_1 n_1 \left(1 - \frac{n_1}{l_1} - f_{12} \frac{n_2}{l_1} \right) \qquad (3)$$

$$\frac{dn_2}{dt} = h_2 n_2 \left(1 - \frac{n_2}{l_2} - f_{21} \frac{n_1}{l_2} \right) \qquad (4)$$

Where h_1, l_1, r_2, l_2, f_{12} and f_{21} are all positive constants and the h_is are the linear birth rates and the l_is are the carrying capacities. The f_{12} and f_{21} measure the competitive effect of n_2 on n_1 and n_1 on n_2 respectively: they are generally not equal.

2.3 Evaluation Parameters

We pose the objective of finding a protocol that can be implemented in a decentralized way by sources and routers, and controls the system to a stable equilibrium point which satisfies some basic requirements: high utilization of network resources, small queues, and a degree of control over resource allocation. All of these are required to be *scalable*, i.e. hold for an arbitrary network, with possibly high capacity and delay. We first specify the design objectives for the *equilibrium point* to be achieved by our system:

1. *Network utilization*: Link equilibrium rates should of course not exceed the capacity *(B)*, but also should attempt to track it. 2. Equilibrium *queues* should be *empty* (or small) to avoid queuing delays and achieve constant RTT. 3. Resource allocation *fairness*: Congested link bandwidth should be allocated fairly among the sources.

Equilibrium considerations are meaningful if the system can operate at or near this point; for this reason we pose as a basic requirement the *stability* of the equilibrium point. Ideally, we would seek global stability from any initial condition, but at the very least, we should require local stability from a neighborhood. This objective is sometimes debated, since instability in the form of oscillations could perhaps be tolerated in the network context, and might be a small price to pay for an aggressive control. In other terms some ones believe that instability in the form of oscillations is better than stability that is realized through an aggressive control.

In summary, network flow control concerns adjustment of individual transmission rates of a number of sources over a set of links, subject to link capacity constraints. The main purpose of flow control is to fully utilize all the links in the network, while at the same time achieving some sort of fairness among the sources. It is also desirable that congestion control system operates in a stable regime.

3 Predator-Prey Approach: Congestion Control Using Predator-Prey Model

In order to clarify the similarity between TCP/AQM[1] congestion control mechanism and predator-prey interaction, we look at the TCP/AQM running on a network: **(1)** In the absence of packet drop (P), congestion window (W) would grow. **(2)** On the occurrence of a packet drop, congestion window size would decline. **(3)** Incoming packet rate contribution to packet drop growth is proportional to available traffic intensity, as well as, the packet drop rate itself. **(4)** In the absence of a packet stream, for sustenance, packet drop rate will decline. We see that this behavior is close to the predator-prey interaction. This similarity motivates us to use predator-prey approach to control population size of W_is. We define two class of predator species that can prey W_is Suppose that there are K species, P_1, P_2, ..., P_k in the congested router. P_i can prey all the W individuals but there can be a weighting preference for P_i to prey W_i several times more significant to all other W_k (k≠i) individuals. A similar relation can also be imagined between "*queue occupancy*" in congested router (q) and "*congestion window size*" (W) of the sources sharing this queue. Hence the interactions of (P, W) and (q, W) has been considered as *predator- prey* interaction.

To specify a congestion control system, it remains to define (i) how the sources adjust their rates based on their aggregate prices (the TCP algorithm), and (ii) how the links adjust their prices and queue size based on their aggregate rates (the AQM algorithm). We can in general postulate a dynamic model of the form

$$\dot{W}_i = F_i(W_i, P_j, q) \qquad j=1,2,...,k$$

$$\dot{P} = G_i(P_i, W_j, q) \qquad j=1,2,...,k$$

$$\dot{q} = H(W_j, q) \qquad j=1,2,...,k$$

Since we adopted predator-prey interaction for population control of W, hence we use generalized Lotka–Volterra predator–prey system to drive F, G an H. This deliberation leads to the following Bio-inspired distributed congestion control algorithms.

$$\frac{dW_i}{dt} = Wi \left[a_i - \sum_{j=1}^{k} b_{ij} P_j - r_i q \right] \qquad (5)$$

$$\frac{dP_i}{dt} = P_i \left[\sum_{j=1}^{k} c_{ij} W_j - d_i \right] \qquad where \quad i=1,...,k \quad (6)$$

$$\frac{dq}{dt} = \left[\sum_{j=1}^{k} e_j W_j - m \right] \qquad (7)$$

---

[1] Active Queue Management.

Whereas the parameters are defined by:

a_i is the growth rate of W_i in the absence of P and q. b_{ji} is the decrement rate per encounter of W_i due to P_j. r is the decrement rate per encounter of W_i due to q. d_i is the decrement rate of P_i in the absence of W, *that we set it to 0.8B/k.* c_{ij} is the efficiency of turning predated W_j into P_i. m is set to $Min(B, q+\sum Wi)$. e_j is the efficiency of turning predated W_j into q that we set it to 1.

In the network context P_is are rate mismatch i.e. difference between input rate and target capacity d_i and q refers to buffer occupancy. The sources use equations (5) to computes its own congestion window size (TCP) and routers use equations (6)-(7) to adjust their P_is and q based on aggregated rates.

3.1 Illustrative Example

In this section, we illustrate the proposed model through of an example. We use a four-connection network, as given in Fig. 2. The network has a single bottleneck link of capacity 50 pkts/*RTT*, shared by 4 sources. All other links have bandwidth of 100 pkt/RTT. All flows are long-lived, and sources always are active It is expected that the proposed method is applicable to solve networks that are more complicated.

According to the proposed model in (5)-(7), we can write the congestion control regime of the test network in the form of equations (8)-(16). According to mathematical biology, in order to establish a stably operated and fairly shared network the effect of self-inhibitive action must be larger than inhibitive action by others [33]. Hence, in equations (8)-(16) any b_{ii} and c_{ii} are several times (in this example 18 times) larger than other b_{ij} and c_{ij} respectively.

$$dW_1 = w_1(1 - 0.9P_1 - 0.05P_2 - 0.05P_3 - 0.05P_4 - 0.02q) \tag{8}$$

$$dP_1 = p_1(0.9W_1 + 0.05W_2 + 0.05W_3 + 0.05W_4 - 10) \tag{9}$$

$$dW_2 = W_2(1 - 0.05P_1 - 0.9P_2 - 0.05P_3 - 0.05P_4 - 0.02q) \tag{10}$$

$$dP_2 = P_2(0.1W_1 + 0.9W_2 + 0.1W_3 + 0.1W_4 - 10) \tag{11}$$

$$dW_3 = W_3(1 - 0.05P_1 - 0.05P_2 - 0.9P_3 - 0.05P_4 - 0.02q) \tag{12}$$

$$dP_3 = p_3(0.05W_1 + 0.05W_2 + 0.9W_3 + 0.05W_4 - 10) \tag{13}$$

$$dW_4 = w_4(1 - 0.05P_1 - 0.05P_2 - 0.05P_3 - 0.9P_4 - 0.02q) \tag{14}$$

$$dP_4 = p_4(0.05W_1 + 0.05W_2 + 0.05W_3 + 0.9W_4 - 10) \tag{15}$$

$$dq = W_1 + W_2 + W_3 + W_4 - \min(50, q + W_1 + W_2 + W_3 + W_4) \tag{16}$$

In order to simulate the test network and assess its behavior, we solve the equations (8)-(16) numerically using Matlab 7.1. We use the following initial state in which each source has different window size:

$W_1(0) = 1,\ W_2(0) = 2,\ W_3(0) = 4,\ W_4(0) = 6,\ P1(0) = P2(0) = P3(0) = P4(0) = 0.1,\ q(0) = 1$

Fig. 5 illustrates the behavior of the sources sharing the bottleneck link. It shows the time curves of the congestion windows size. Fig. 6 illustrates the behavior of the congested link and shows the evolution of marked packets counts. The throughputs of bottleneck link, has been given in Fig. 7.a. This throughput refers to the aggregated loads of all the sources in the bottleneck link. In Fig. 7.b we can find the queue size of the congested router. Evaluation of proposed model is done from the following perspectives.

Fairness- There are several ways of defining and reaching fairness in a network, each one leading to a different allocation of link capacities [34, 35]. We are talking here about fairness in the sharing of the bandwidth of the bottleneck link regardless of the volume of resources consumed by a connection on the other links of the network. This kind of fairness is called, in the literature, the max-min fairness. Other types of fairness however exist, where the objective is to share not only the resources at the bottleneck, but also the resources in other parts of the network.

According to the simulation results in Fig.s 5 and 6, the average throughput and packets mark counts for each source can be summarized as in the table 1:

Table 1. Average throughput and packet mark rate of predator-prey mode

	Source 1	Source 2	Source 3	Source 4
Average throughput (pkt/RTT)	10.4146	10.4365	10.4641	10.4196
Average marked packets count (pkt/RTT)	1.0626	1.0496	1.0668	1.0515

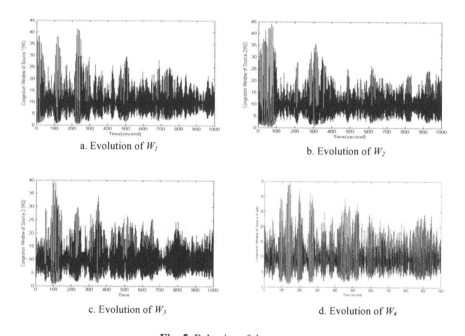

a. Evolution of W_1

b. Evolution of W_2

c. Evolution of W_3

d. Evolution of W_4

Fig. 5. Behavior of the sources

This table shows that in spite of inequality of initial states, all sources enjoy same amount of bandwidth of the bottleneck link and the proposed model satisfies the fairness metric.

Performance-In addition to the prevention of congestion collapse and concerns about fairness, a third reason for a flow to use end-to-end congestion control can be to optimize its own performance regarding throughput, utilization, and loss. Throughput can be measured as a router-based metric of aggregate link throughput, as a flow-based

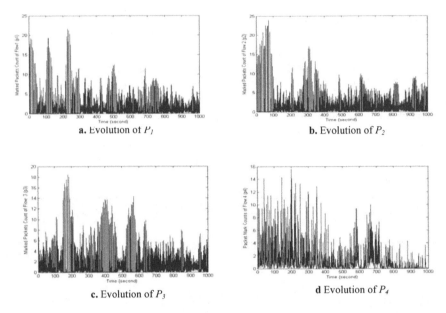

a. Evolution of P_1 **b.** Evolution of P_2

c. Evolution of P_3 **d** Evolution of P_4

Fig. 6. Marked packets counts trace

metric of per-connection transfer times, and as user-based metrics of utility functions. It is a clear goal of most congestion control mechanisms to maximize throughput, subject to application demand and to the constraints of the other metrics.

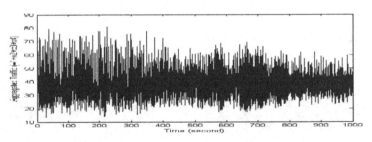

a. Evolution of aggregated traffic of the sources on the link

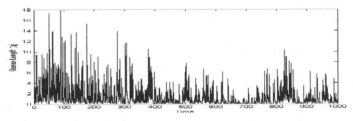

b. Evolution of queue length in congested router (q)

Fig. 7. Aggregated traffic and queue trace

In most occasions, it might be sufficient to consider the aggregated throughput only. In this example, simulation results show that the aggregated traffic is *41.7348 pkt/RTT*. This throughput refers over *80%* utilization on the bottleneck link. According to the report of *AT&T* research group, utilization levels in Internet links are routinely around 70% during the peak hours [36]. So, the achieved utilization in this model is good enough. Fig. 7.b, on the other hand, shows that if we set the queue capacity of the congested router around 20 packets then we roughly wouldn't have any packet loss. The small size of queue length, also, leads to low jitter and low delay for those connections that share this queue capacity.

***Stability*-**In fact, instability can cause three problems. First, it increases jitters in source rate and delay and can be detrimental to some applications. Second, it subjects short-duration connections, which are typically delay and loss sensitive, to unnecessary delay and loss. Finally, it can lead to under-utilization of network links if queues jump between empty and full [4].

From the differential equation viewpoint, one usually looks at a steady state point and wants to know what happens if one starts close to it. A fixed point x_0 of $f(x)$ is called stable if for any given neighborhood $U(x_0)$ there exists another neighborhood $V(x_0) \subseteq U(x_0)$ such that any solution starting in $V(x_0)$ remains in $U(x_0)$ for all $t > 0$. A stability analysis about the steady state is equivalent to the phase plane analysis. Typically, analysis of linear stability can be carried out using community matrix (in ecological context) and its eigenvalues examination [31], but in order to simplify we

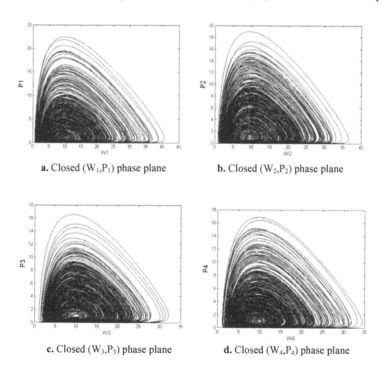

a. Closed (W_1,P_1) phase plane   **b.** Closed (W_2,P_2) phase plane

c. Closed (W_3,P_3) phase plane   **d.** Closed (W_4,P_4) phase plane

Fig. 8. Closed phase plane trajectory for (Wi, Pi)

use the numerical solution of equations (8)-(16) and use phase-plane approach for stability discussion. Fig. 8 shows the closed (W_i, P_i) phase plane trajectories.

Let us examine a little more carefully the results given in Fig. 8. First, note that the direction of time arrows in Fig. 8 is clockwise. This is reflected in Fig. 5 and Fig. 6. Thus all of the trajectories converge roughly around the point (10.4,1.0), and so have a plausible stability near this point. This stability is similar to spiral stability in the context of ordinary differential equations [32].

Fig. 7.a, on the other hand, shows an interesting behavior of the aggregated traffic. This figure. shows that the aggregated traffic has decreasing oscillation level and converges to 43 pkt/RTT. Convergence of aggregated traffic is more obvious than any individual source rate in Fig. 5. This means that because of a global coordination between the sources, the overall behavior of the network has more stability than any of the sources. Fig. 7.b shows that the queue length of congested router approaches to less than 5 packets. Hence, not only the evolution of queue length has a stable regime but also short queue length leads to decrement of delay and jitter in the source rates.

4 Hybrid Approach: Congestion Control Using Combination of Competition and Predator-Prey Models

In order to define a complex system precisely, we should consider all of the involved processes and relation among them. By this motivation, we consider the competition effects between the network users and develop a new equation that addresses another perspective of congestion control problem. Essentially the network users are competitive in the sense that they want to dominate network resources in order to maximize the individual's QoS (Quality of Service) during its communication. In analogy it can be said that *"all of the W_i species that share the bottleneck link incorporate in inter- specie and intra-specie competition in order to maximize their own share of link bandwidth"*. Using equations (3)-(4), this competition can be described by the equation (17).

$$\frac{dW_i}{dt} = h_i W_i \left[1 - \sum_{j=1}^{k} f_{ij} \frac{W_j}{l_i} \right] \qquad where \ i=1,...,k \qquad (17)$$

Where the h_is are the linear birth rates and the l_is are the carrying capacities. The f_{ij}s measure the competitive effect of W_j on W_i.

In order to develop a hybrid mathematical model that include both predation and competition effects we combine the equations (5), (6), (7) and (17). This integration can be described by equation (18)-(20).

$$\frac{dW_i}{dt} = W_i \left[h_i - \sum_{j=1}^{k} b_{ij} p_j - r_i q - \sum_{j=1}^{k} f_{ij} \frac{W_j}{l_i} \right] \qquad (18)$$

$$\frac{dP_i}{dt} = P_i \left[\sum_{j=1}^{k} c_{ij} w_j - d_i \right] \qquad where \ i=1,...,k \qquad (19)$$

$$\frac{dq}{dt} = \left[\sum_{j=1}^{k} e_j w_j - m \right] \qquad (20)$$

Where the h_is, the l_is, the f_{ij}s, the b_{ij}s, the c_{ij}s, the d_is and m are defined such as in equations (5)-(7) and (17).

These equations say that W_i population has multiplicative increase with coefficient of h_i, but this growth will be inhibited by two factors: predation by P and competition with W_j.

4.1 Illustrative Example

According to the equations (18)-(20), we can write the congestion control regime of the test network of the Fig. 2, in the form of equations (21)-(29).

$$dW_1 = W_1(1 - 0.9P_1 - 0.05P_2 - 0.05P_3 - 0.05P_4 - 0.02q - (1.2W_1 + W_2 + W_3 + W_4)/50) \quad (21)$$

$$dP_1 = P_1(0.9W_1 + 0.05W_2 + 0.05W_3 + 0.05W_4 - 10) \quad (22)$$

$$dW_2 = W_2(1 - 0.05P_1 - 0.9P_2 - 0.05P_3 - 0.05P_4 - 0.02q - (W_1 + 1.2W_2 + W_3 + W_4)/50) \quad (23)$$

$$dP_2 = P_2(0.1W_1 + 0.9W_2 + 0.1W_3 + 0.1W_4 - 10) \quad (24)$$

$$dW_3 = W_3(1 - 0.05P_1 - 0.05P_2 - 0.9P_3 - 0.05P_4 - 0.02q - (W_1 + W_2 + 1.2W_3 + W_4)/50) \quad (25)$$

$$dP_3 = P_3(0.05W_1 + 0.05W_2 + 0.9W_3 + 0.05W_4 - 10) \quad (26)$$

$$dW_4 = W_4(1 - 0.05P_1 - 0.05P_2 - 0.05P_3 - 0.9P_4 - 0.02q - (W_1 + W_2 + W_3 + 1.2W_4)/50) \quad (27)$$

$$dP_4 = P_4(0.05W_1 + 0.05W_2 + 0.05W_3 + 0.9W_4 - 10) \quad (28)$$

$$dq = W_1 + W_2 + W_3 + W_4 - min(50, \ q + W_1 + W_2 + W_3 + W_4) \quad (29)$$

In this case, again P_is are the marked packet counts in the flow i, q is length of queue in the congested router, and W_i is congestion window size for source i. As mentioned in the previous section, in order to establish a stably operated and fairly shared network the effect of self-inhibitive action must be larger than inhibitive action by others. Hence, in Equations (25-33) any b_{ii} and c_{ii} are several times (in this example 18 times) larger than other b_{ij} and c_{ij} respectively.

In order to simulate the test network and assess its behavior, we solve the equations (21)-(29) numerically, again using Matlab 7.1. We use the following initial state in which each source has different window size.

$$P1(0) = P2(0) = P3(0) = P4(0) = 0.1, \ q(0) = 1, \ W_1(0) = 1, \ W_2(0) = 2, \ W_3(0) = 4, \ W_4(0) = 6$$

Fig. 9 illustrates the behavior of the sources sharing the bottleneck link. It shows the time curves of the congestion window size for any source. After a transient phase, all of the W_is converge to a constant value. Fig. 10 shows the evolution of marked packet counts in the congested router. The throughputs of bottleneck link, has been given in Fig. 11.a. This throughput refers to aggregate loads of all of the sources in the bottleneck link $(W_1 + W_2 + W_3 + W_4)$. In Fig. 11.b we can find the

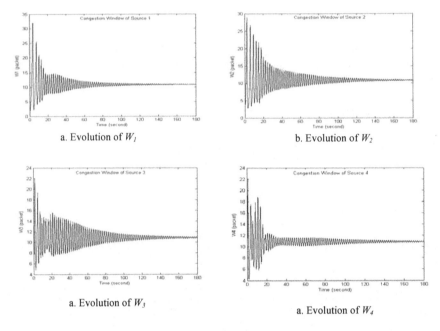

a. Evolution of W_1

b. Evolution of W_2

a. Evolution of W_3

a. Evolution of W_4

Fig. 9. The sources behavior

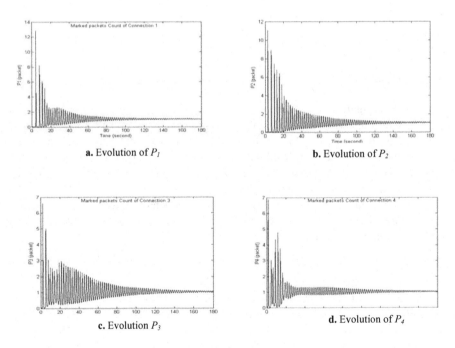

a. Evolution of P_1

b. Evolution of P_2

c. Evolution P_3

d. Evolution of P_4

Fig. 10. Marked packets counts trace

queue size of congested router. This queue size achieved through the $dq = w_1 + w_2 + w_3 + w_4 - min(50, \quad q + w_1 + w_2 + w_3 + w_4)$.

In order to reference to the results of Figs. 9-12, we note that:

1. As we can see in Fig.s 9, 10 and 12, the source rates and the link prices (marking probability) track more stable behavior in compare to the predator-prey approach. In their steady state, there is no oscillation, and the speed of convergence to this steady state is more accelerated than predator-prey approach.

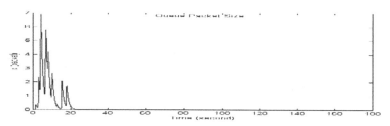

a. Evolution of aggregated loads of the sources

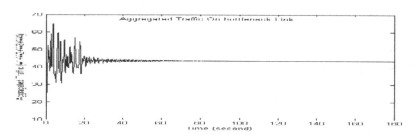

b. Evolution of queue occupancy (q) in congested router

Fig. 11. Aggregate traffic and queue trace

Tabel 2. Average throughput and packets mark rate of Hybrid model

	Source 1	Source 2	Source 3	Source 4
Average throughput (pkt/RTT)	10.88	10.88	10.87	10.88
Average marked packets count (pkt/RTT)	1.015	1.019	1.023	1.026

2. Fairness is achieved: at each equilibrium stage, the bandwidth is shared equally among sources despite their heterogeneous initial state. Table 2 shows this fact.

3. The queue size is zero in equilibrium and around 3 packets (less than 0.1 RTT of queuing delay) in transient. This can be found in Fig. 11.a.

4. According to the Fig. 11.b, after the startup transient of the first sources, bottleneck link utilization remains always around the 90%.

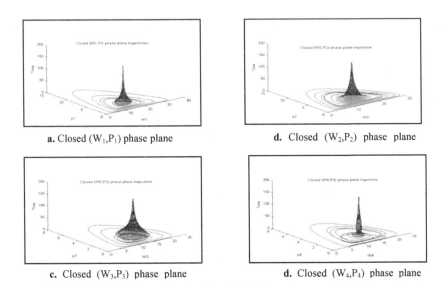

a. Closed (W_1, P_1) phase plane   **d.** Closed (W_2, P_2) phase plane

c. Closed (W_3, P_3) phase plane   **d.** Closed (W_4, P_4) phase plane

Fig. 12. Closed phase plane trajectory for (W_i, P_i)

5 Implementation Issues

There are a number of issues, which need to be dealt with in considering the implementation of the BICC. According to the differential equations (18)-(20), BICC suggests treating the congested link and sources as a processor in a distributed computing system. In BICC during each RTT any source needs to know the queue size, q, marked packets counts $(P_1, P_2, \dots)$ and link utilization, u $((W_1+W_2+W_3+\dots)/B)$. Using this information, any source computes its own congestion window size. For instance, in the last example, source 1 receives P_1, P_2, P_3, P_4, q *and* u from congested router, and then uses equation (21) to update its congestion window size for the next RTT. On the other hand, the congested router must compute the new queue size and mark rates. Links must have access to their weighted aggregate flow ($\Sigma c_i W_i$); this quantity is not directly known, but can be estimated from arriving packets. It receives W_i from all sources and then updates mark rates P_i and q.

We remember that AQM component of BICC computes $pric_i = \sum_j b_{ij} p_j + r_i q$ as total measured congestion for flow i. To communicate $price_i$ to source i the technique of random exponential marking [38] can be used. For dissemination of $price_i$, an ECN [37] bit would be marked at the congested link with probability $pm_i = 1 - \phi^{-price_i}$ $whre\, \phi > 1$. Assuming independence, the overall probability that a packet from source i gets marked is $1 - \phi^{-price_i}$, and therefore $price_i$ can be estimated from marking statistics at each source. This price is used by source i for adjusting its sending rate. We make two remarks on implementation. First, BICC uses only local information. So this system works in a decentralized fashion. Second, such as REM [38], BICC can use the sum of the link prices along a multiple congested links as a measure of congestion in the *path* and to embed it into the *end-to-end* marking probability that can be observed at the sources.

The following algorithm summarizes the implementation process.

BICC Algorithm: Hybrid Approach

Congested router's algorithm:

At time RTT,2RTT,3RTT,... congested router:

1- Receives W_s packet from all sources $s \in S$ that goes through bottle link l.

2- Computes a new queue length and a new mark rate for all sources that use link l.

$$\frac{dP_i}{dt} = P_i \left[\sum_{j=1}^{k} c_{ij} w_j - d_i \right] \quad where \quad i = 1,...,k$$

$$\frac{dq}{dt} = \left[\sum_{j=1}^{k} e_{ij} w_j - m \right]$$

3-   Computes marking probability pm_i through

$$price_i = \sum_{j=1}^{k} b_{ij} p_j + r_i q$$

$$pm_i = 1 - \phi^{-price_i} \quad whre \ \phi > 1$$

3- Uses ECN to communicate the new mark rates (pm_i).for all the sources that use link l.

Source i's algorithm:

At time RTT,2RTT,3RTT,... source i:

1- Receives from the congested router marked packets and computes pm_i.

2- Estimates from marking statistics the $price_i$:

$$price_i = -\log_\phi^{(1-pm_i)}$$

3- Choose a new window size for the next period:

$$\frac{dW_i}{dt} = Wi[h_i - Price]$$

We leave the algorithm of predator-prey approach because of its similarity to hybrid approach.

6   How Does System Biology Benefit from This Contribution?

Systems biology is an emergent field that aims at system-level understanding of biological systems. Cybernetics, for example, aims at describing animals from the control and communication theory. System biology can be summarized as: (1) understanding of structure of the system, such as gene regulatory and biochemical networks, as well as physical structures, (2) understanding of dynamics of the system, both quantitative and qualitative analysis as well as construction of theory/model with powerful prediction capability, (3) understanding of control methods of the system, and (4) understanding of design methods of the system, are key milestones to judge how much we understand the system.

From top view our mapping directs biologists to use the theories and the results of researches in the area of communication network that is one of the most active research areas. Especially since biological systems have networked structures it is quite easy to show very close similarity between biology and communication networks. By mapping the network theories biologist can develop new theories for study, analysis and control of biological systems. For example due to our contribution in this paper the population control tactics of the nature are very analogous to congestion control tactics in communication networks. Hence, it is possible to apply the current congestion control algorithms in some biologic applications such as pest population control. It is also possible to use the models and algorithms of congestion control for modeling and studying the population dynamics from other perspectives.

7   Conclusion Remarks

We have argued that Internet is a new biologic environment for human kind. One of the benefits of this view is bio-inspired algorithms that gain from exploiting more sophisticated biological models, and from being based on sound analytical principles. We believe that biology could benefit from the resulting sophisticated models, too. We have outlined what we believe to be a suitable conceptual framework including these various components. We have suggested how BICC models might fit into this framework. We have used a model based on predator-prey interaction to design a congestion control mechanism in communication network and have seen that with some consideration on parameters, this model leads to a relatively stable, fair and high performance congestion control algorithm. Then we combined predator-prey model with competition model. This hybrid model causes more stability, fairness and performance in compare with predator-prey approach.

Although the experimental results indelicate the credibility of proposed models, but a number of avenues for future extensions remains. First, in this paper we didn't study the impact of different *RTT*, it is one of the central parts of the future works. Second, with mathematical characterization of network objective such as fairness, stability and etc. we can use mathematical rules for setting of parameters of purposed model to achieve well-designed communication network.

References

1. Jacobson, v.: Congestion avoidance and control, ACM Computer Communication Review (1988)
2. Richard Stevens, W.: TCP/IP illustrated, vol. 1: the protocols, Addison Wesley (1994)
3. Pagano, M., Secchi, R.: A Survey on TCP Performance Evaluation and Modeling (2004)
4. Wang, J.: A Theoretical Study of Internet Congestion Control: Equilibrium and Dynamics, PhD thesis, university of Caltech (2005)
5. Floyd, S.: Connections with multiple congested gateways in packet-switched networks part 1: One-way traffic, Computer Communications Review (1991)
6. Lakshman, T.V., Madhow, U.: The performance of TCP/IP for networks with high bandwidth-delay products and random loss, IFIP Transactions (1994)
7. Ott, T., Kemperman, J., Mathis, M.: The stationary behavior of ideal TCP congestion avoidance (1998)

8. Mathis, M., Semke, J., Mahdavi, J., Ott, T.: The macroscopic behavior of the TCP congestion avoidance algorithm, Computer Communication Review (1997)
9. Padhye, J., Firoiu, V., Towsley, D., Kurose, J.: Modeling TCP Reno performance: A simple model and its empirical validation, IEEE/ACM Transactions on Networking (2000)
10. Handley, M., Floyd, S., Padhye, J., Widmer, J.: TCP Friendly, Rate Control (TFRC): Protocol specification, RFC 3168, Internet Engineering Task Force (2003),
11. Misra, V., Gong, W., Towsley, D.: Stochastic differential equation modeling and analysis of tcp-window size behavior (1999)
12. Misra, V., Gong, W., Towsley, D.: Fluid-based analysis of a network of AQM routers supporting TCP flows with an application to RED, ACM Sigcomm (2000)
13. Hollot, C., Misra, V., Towsley, D., Gong, W.: A control theorietic analysis of RED, IEEE Infocom (2001)
14. Low, S.H., Paganini, F., Wang, J., Doyle, J.C.: Linear stability of TCP/RED and a scalable control. Computer Networks Journal (2003)
15. Aweya, J., Ouellette, M., Montuno, D.Y.: A control theoretic approach to active queue management. Computer Networks (2001)
16. Hollot, C., Misra, V., Towsley, D., Gong, W.: On designing improved controller for AQM routers supporting TCP flows. IEEE Infocom (2001)
17. Kim, K.B., Low, S.H.: Analysis and design of aqm for stabilizing tcp. Technical Report Caltech CSTR 2002009, Caltech (2002)
18. Zhang, H., Baohong, L., Dou, W.: Design of a robust active queue management algorithm based on feedback compensation. ACM Sigcomm (2003)
19. Ryu, S., Rump, C., Qiao, C.: Advances in active queue management(AQM) based TCP congestion control. Telecommunication System (2004)
20. Choe, H., Low, S.H.: Stabilized Vegas, IEEE Infocom (2003)
21. Low, S.H., Peterson, L., Wang, L.: Understanding Vegas: a duality model. Journal of ACM (2002)
22. Jin, C., Wei, D.X., Low, S.H.: FAST TCP: motivation, architecture, algorithms, performance. IEEE Infocom (2004)
23. Wang, J., Wei, D.X., Low, S.H.: Modeling and stability of FAST TCP. IEEE Infocom (2005)
24. Kelly, F.: Charging and rate control for elastic traffic, European Transactions on Telecommunications (1997)
25. Kelly, F.P., Maulloo, A., Tan, D.: Rate, control for communication networks: Shadow prices, proportional fairness and stability. Journal of Operations Research Society (1998)
26. Low, S.H., Lapsley, D.E.: Optimization flow control I: basic algorithm and convergence. IEEE/ACM Transactions on Networking (1999)
27. Elizabeth, S.: Mathematical Models in Biology: An Introduction. Cambridge press, Cambridge (2003)
28. Lotka, A.: Elements of Physical Biology, Williams and Wilkins, Baltimore (1925)
29. Floyd, S., Van Jacobson,: Random early detection gateways for congestion avoidance. IEEE/ACM Transactions on Networking (1993)
30. Mathis, M., Mahdavi, J., Floyd, S., Romanow, A.: TCP Selective Acknowledgement Options. RFC 2018 (1996)
31. Murray, J.D.: Mathematical Biology: I. an Introduction, 3rd edn. Springer, Heidelberg (2002)
32. Simmons, G.f.: differential equations (with applications and historical notes). McGraw-Hill Inc, New York (1972)

33. Murata, M.: Biologically Inspired Communication Network Control, International Workshop onSelf-* Properties in Complex Information Systems (2004)
34. Kelly, F.: Mathematical Modeling of the Internet, Mathematics Unlimited-2001 and Beyond. Springer, Berlin (2001)
35. Analoui, M., Jamali, Sh.: TCP Fairness Enhancement Through a parametric Mathematical Model, CCSP2005, IEEE International Conference. IEEE Computer Society Press, Los Alamitos (2005)
36. Odlyzko, A.: The low utilization and high cost of data networks, AT&T Labs - Research, http://www.dtc.umn.edu/odlyzko/doc/high.network.cost.pdf.
37. Ramakrishna, K., Floyd, S., Black, D.: The addition of explicit congestion noti-fication (ECN) to IP, RFC 3168, Internet Engineering Task Force (2001)

Computational Thinking in Biology

Corrado Priami

The Microsoft Research - University of Trento
Centre for Computational and Systems Biology
priami@cosbi.eu

Abstract. The paper presents a new approach based on process calculi
to systems modeling suitable for biological systems. The main character-
istic of process calculi is a linguistic description level to define incrementally and compositionally executable models. The formalism is suitable
to be exploited on the same system at different levels of abstractions
connected through well defined formal rules. The abstraction principle
that represents biological entities as interacting computational units is
the basis of the computational thinking that can help biology to unravel
the functions of the cell machinery. We discuss then the perspectives that
process calculi can open to life sciences and the impact that this can in
turn produce on computer science.

1 Introduction

Systems level understanding of phenomena has recently become an issue in biology. The complexity of molecular interactions (gene regulatory networks, signaling pathways, metabolic networks, etc.) makes impossible to handle the emergent
behavior of systems simply by putting together the behavior of their components. Interaction is a key point in the study of emergence and complexity in
any field and hence in biology as well where the molecular machinery inside a
cell determines the behavior of complex organisms.

Besides interaction, the other key issue to develop computer-based tools for
systems biology is incremental construction of models. We need to add something
to a model once new knowledge is available without altering what we already
did. This is an essential feature for modeling formalisms being applicable to real
size problems (not only in the biological applicative domain). Many approaches
have been investigated in the literature to model and simulate biological systems
(e.g., ODE or stochastic differential equations, Petri nets, boolean networks,
agent-based systems), but most of them suffer limitations with respect to the
above issues.

In recent times, programming languages based approaches have been proposed to generate executable models at a linguistic level. We think that they
are a suitable tool to address interaction, incremental building of models and
complexity of emergent behavior. As usual in computer science, the definition
of a high level linguistic formalism that then must be mapped onto lower level
representations to be executed may loose efficiency but gain a lot in expressive

C. Priami (Ed.): Trans. on Comput. Syst. Biol. VIII, LNBI 4780, pp. 63–76, 2007.

power and usability. Being the systems in hand huge, we need such formalisms to minimize the error prone activity of specifying behavior.

The main idea is that computer networks, and Internet in particular, are the artificial systems most similar to biological systems. Languages developed in the last twenty years to study and predict quantitatively the dynamic evolution of these networks could be of help in modeling and analysing biological systems. Recent results show that process calculi (very simple modeling languages including the basic feature to model interaction of components) have been successfully adopted to develop simulators [22,24,19] that can faithfully represent biological behavior.

The correspondence between the way in which computer scientists attacked the complexity of artificial systems and the way in which such complexity is emerging in biology when interpreting living systems as information processing unit [13] is very strict. Therefore computational thinking [26] is a tool that can extremely help enhance our understanding of living systems dynamics. Computational thinking expresses the attitude of looking at the same problem at different levels of abstraction and to model it through executable formalisms that can provide insights on temporal evolution of the problem in hand. Therefore the basic feature of computational thinking is abstraction of reality in such a way that the neglected details in the model make it executable by a machine. Of course, different executable abstractions of the same problem exist and the choice is driven by the properties to be investigated. Indeed, science history shows us that a single model for the whole reality does not exist: our modeling activity must be driven by the properties of the phenomenon under investigation that we want to look at.

Process calculi have been originally introduced [15,12] as specification languages for distributed software systems. The specification can be refined towards an actual implementation within the same formalism. Any refinement step is validated by formal proofs of correctness. This approach is a good example of a framework that imposes the application of the computational thinking and therefore we work on it to obtain a similar framework for biological systems.

We here briefly and intuitively introduce process calculi (in particular we concentrate on the β-language) to show on an example how they can be used to model biological systems. We then investigate the potential of the approach in a perspective vision. We first discuss how life scientists can improve their performance by relying on software and conceptual tools that allow them to mimick the standard activities they perform in wet labs. There are however two main advantages to work in silico: speed and cost. Actually experiments last few minutes instead of hours or days and the cost is extremely reduced. Once the scientist think of having something concrete in silico can move towards the wet lab and test *in practice* the hypotheses. Essentially there is an iterative loop between in silico production of hypothesis and wet testing of them.

The longer term perspective of the approach is related to enhancement of computer science. The knowledge we gain from developing linguistic mechanisms to describe and execute the dynamics of complex biological systems could lead to the definition of a new generation of programming languages and new programming paradigms that can enhance the software production tools now available.

2   Abstracting Biological Systems

A biological system can be studied at the molecular, cellular, tissue, organ and population levels. The dynamic steps that drive the state change of the above systems can be always reduced to interactions of some kind (e.g., protein-protein, cell-cell, member-member, etc.). Actually, one of the most used concepts in systems level understanding of biology is the one of network (see Fig. 1): a structure made up of nodes (the components of the considered system) linked by arcs (the interactions between components). The interaction can enhance or inhibit some activities, thus we usually observe activation arcs (ending with an arrow) and repressor arcs (ending with a line orthogonal to the arc).

A reasonable formalisms able to model the dynamics of biological systems must then be able to represent components and their interactions. Since networks are essentially graphs whose arcs represent some kind of chemical/physical reaction between components, a mathematical tool to represent the system could be

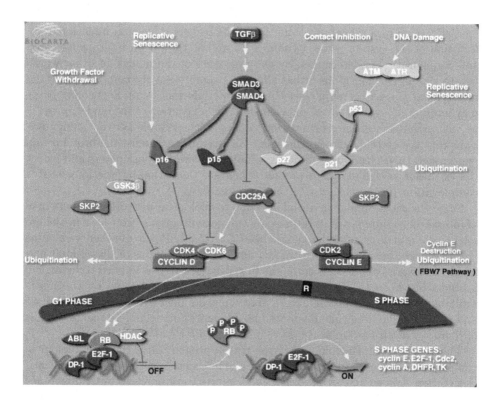

Fig. 1. A cell cycle pathway from the Biocarta database

a stoichiometric matrix [17]. Rows and columns are components, the entries store some quantitative measure characterizing the interaction of the corresponding components. Although the matrix contains all the relevant information, its size is extremely large for practical useful systems.

Computer science, executable, formalisms that resemble the stoichiometric matrix are the ones based on multi-set rewriting (e.g., P systems [18,5] or variant of Petri Nets, e.g., [10]). The main limitation of the stoichiometric matrix as well as of these computer science formalisms is that they need to represent in the description of the model all the possible configuration in which the network can pass and all the possible interactions explicitly. No emergent behavior can arise from the execution or the analysis of the model if it has not been explicitly modeled.

Since biological networks exhibit combinatorial features, i.e., the number of possible configurations of the network grows exponentially with respect to the number of components, the explicit representation of all the configurations is a difficult, time-consuming and error-prone task. Summing up the approaches mentioned above are mainly used and suitable to systematize the knowledge on dynamics of systems and to make it unambiguous. The main applications are then storing and comparison of models.

Another important feature of models is however the predicting power that can help designing new experiments to discover new knowledge. To stress the heuristic value of a model, we think that it is better to have an intentional description of the system whose dynamics as well as the set on intermediate step and configuration is determined by the execution of the model. In other words we are looking for a formalism that allows us to represent the components of the network and a set of general rules that provide information on how components may interact. Then, "in silico" experiments (i.e., execution of the model) provide us with possible scenarios of interaction (i.e., with possible network configurations that the system can pass through). As an example, we list the proteins in a system and their slectivity/affinity or binding/unbinding parameters and we let the execution of the model to predict which are the actual interactions and/or complexation/decomplexation of the proteins.

Since the most similar artificial systems to biological networks are networks of interacting computer or of interacting software programs, we re-use in the life science domain description languages like CCS [15], CSP [12] and then π-calculus [16] that have been invented to model and study properties of distributed and mobile software systems. Actually, the first process calculus applied to biological problem has been the stochastic π-calculus [20] (also supported by automatic available tools for simulation [22,19]) that opened a field of research that is more and more populated of calculi adopted for biological modeling. To mention a few of them we recall BioAmbients [23], CCS-R [6], PEPA [1].

The abstraction principle underlying this approach [24] is that any biological component is represented by a program. The interaction between biological entities is then represented as an exchange of information between programs. Since in a distributed software system in which many programs run simultaneously the information exchanged between them makes the future behavior of the system change, the interaction becomes the basic step of state change exactly as it happens in biological networks. We slightly refine this principle by equipping communication links with types that define the sensitivity of the biological component they belong to (see Fig. 2).

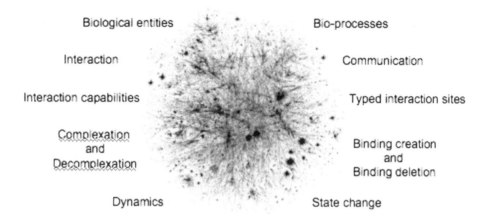

Biological entities

Bio-processes

Interaction

Communication

Interaction capabilities

Typed interaction sites

Complexation
and
Decomplexation

Binding creation
and
Binding deletion

Dynamics

State change

Fig. 2. Abstraction principles to model biological systems - figure prepared by A. Romanel and L. Dematté

The linguistic level of the calculi allows us to have representations that grow linearly with the number of components of the net, while only the execution of the model faces the exponential number of configurations that the network can reach. The selection of the next state from the current configuration is driven by the quantities that express the affinity of interaction through the implementation of a stochastic run-time engine based on the Gillespie's algorithm [9]. Therefore, the execution of a model provide us with the variation over time of the concentration of the components that form the system, i.e., the execution of a model corresponds to the stochastic simulation of the system.

The other property that makes process calculi good candidates to overcome the actual limitations of modeling approaches is the so-called *compositionality* or capability to build models incrementally. Most of the current approaches allow to increase the size of a model by adding new knowledge to it and performing a partial rewriting of the current available model (think of ODE when adding new variables, or rewriting systems when adding new interacting elements – one needs to take care of the new comers variables or components in the existing equations or rewriting rules). This is clearly an obstacle to the scalability of the approach towards genome-size and organism applications. Since the combinatoric features of networks are handled in process calculi at execution time, the description of new elements can be implemented just by adding to the pool of already existing programs the new one describing the new biological entity and by adding to the affinity rules the values describing the interacting capabilities of the new entity. Then the run-time engine will take care of the new program according to its interaction capabilities. This is common practice in software development where *interfaces* of programs are defined to let them interact without the need of re-coding their internal structure. As an example see Fig. 3 where the interface of the β-workbench introduced in the next section is reported. The rectangles represent the bio-processes, i.e. the biological elements, and the arcs their interaction capabilities. Adding new elements to the system is just a matter of introducing a new box with the corresponding interaction arcs. The code generator will then take care of the new possible behavior of the overall system.

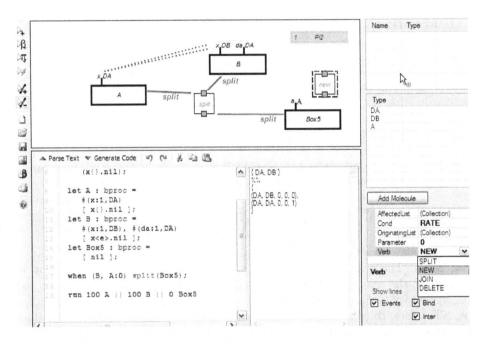

Fig. 3. The modeling interface (β-designer) of the β-workbench

Most of the process calculi mentioned above have been applied to biological problems although they have been defined for computer science modeling. The result was a feasibility study of the potentials of these calculi to model and simulate biological systems. At the same time some limitations emerged at the modeling level. Hence, many researchers defined new variants and extensions of the existing calculi to directly address biological features. Among them we mention the Brane calculi [2] designed to model membrane interactions, the κ-calculus [7] designed to model complexation and decomplexation, SPICO [14] designed to add object-oriented features to stochastic π-calculus, β-binders [21] designed to exploit the notion of interface of biological entities and introduce a sensitivity/affinity based interaction. In fact all the calculi defined before β-binders have been implicitly assuming that two structures can interact only if they are exactly complementary (a perfect key-lock mechanism of interaction). Besides stochastic π-calculus, β binders is the only process calculus equipped with a stochastic simulation engine [25]. Since β binders is the last process calculus defined and enjoys properties that the previous proposals do not have, in the next section we introduce the basics of process calculi relying on β binders.

3   The β Workbench

We present in this section a frame to model and simulate biological systems relying on process calculi. The β workbench (hereafter βWB) is based on *beta binders* and it is made up of three components: the β language with its stochastic abstract machine, the β designer (see Fig. 3) to help modeling activities and the β plotter (see Fig. 4) to inspect the results of the simulations. Since the purpose of the paper is to illustrate the perspectives of applying process calculi in modeling biological systems, we concentrate here only on the β language and we refer the reader to [25] for more details on the βWB.

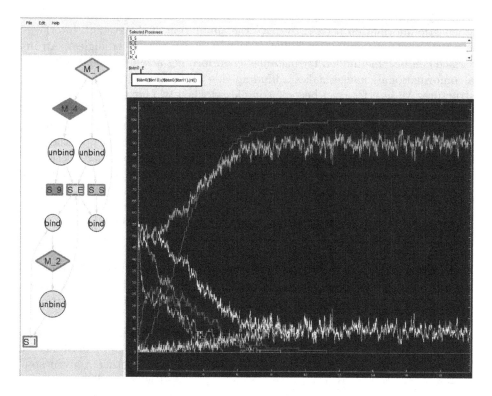

Fig. 4. The output interface (β-plotter) of the β-workbench

Every biological entity is represented as a box (e.g. a protein, a cell, a member of a population) with a set of interfaces through which the entity interacts with other entities (e.g. a set of receptors). Any box contains a small program describing the activities that the box can perform in response to stimuli on its interfaces (e.g., conformational changes, activation or deactivation of other interfaces). A whole biological system is composed of a set of boxes (proteins, cells, populations) each of them equipped with a unique name (species) and an arity determining the available numbers or concentration of biological entities abstracted by the box in the system. Note that a box can pass through different states according to the configurations of its interfaces and its internal program without the need of changing its unique name (species) in the model. For instance, Fig. 6(a) represents graphically a box where b_1 is the unique name of the box and 17 is the number of the copies of the box available in the system (the concentration of the corresponding component); P inside the box is its internal program (how the box works in response to stimuli on interfaces); and rectangles, triangles and circles on the border of the box are the interfaces. The color of an interface denotes its type, while x_i denotes its name and s_i is the stochastic parameter describing a continuous time exponential distributions. The type of an interface is used to determine the affinity of interaction between boxes. In fact the run time engine is based on a function α between types that provides a quantity expressing the propensity of interaction. Finally the parameter s_i is a stochastic information needed to drive the simulation of the system. Interfaces can be active (rectangles), or hidden (circles) or complexed (triangles). An interface can become hidden for instance when forming a complex that following a conformational change makes a binding side hidden by its three dimensional structure. An interface can become complexed when two boxes glue together by that interface.

The actions that a box can perform are either internal to a box (monomolecular operations), or they affect two boxes (bimolecular operations) or they are driven by global conditions on the system (events). Monomolecular operations manipulates interfaces through hiding and unhiding, creating new interfaces or changing the types (i.e., interaction capabilities) of existing interfaces. Furthermore they may allow interaction between different part of the same box or may decide to kill the box. These operations are graphically represented in Fig. 6(b). Bimolecular operations involve two boxes and allow them to interact. Interaction is implemented via exchange of information between the two boxes or via complexation or decomplexation of interfaces. The speed and probability of interaction is driven by the affinity function over the types of the interfaces selected for the current interaction. These operations are graphically depicted in Fig. 6(c).

Events are global rules of the execution environment triggered by conditions such as comparison with threshold on concentrations of boxes or existence of a given species in the current state. We can also check whether a given step or simulation time is reached. The actions associated with conditions can be deletion or creation of boxes, joining of two boxes into one or the splitting of a a box into two. The notion of event inherited from event-based programming allow us to control the context in which the phenomenon under investigation is happening. Furthermore, events easily allows us to perturbate the system modeled and to analyse the new behavior. Perturbation of models is an essential feature if we want to develop an in-silico lab. In fact most of the experiments are the observation of the reactions of a system to some pre-defined perturbations.

The selection of the actions to be performed is driven by the Gillespie's algorithm in connection with the flow of control of boxes coded in their internal programs.

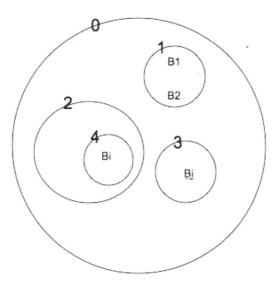

Fig. 5. Hierarchical structures. Compartments are uniquely identified by sequences of natural numbers. The largest one is identified by 0 and it contains three comparments identified by 02, 01 and 03. Furthermore, the compartment 02 contains the compartment 024.

Due to the large number of membranes existing in biological systems, an important feature to model real case studies is the ability of expressing compartments. The need of adding spatial information to models is also in computer science when modeling distributed software systems. For instance, it is important to partition a system into administrative domains to associate privileges with them and to check security polices. Two approaches have been adopted in process calculi: explicit representation of domains into hierarchical structures as in the ambient-family calculi [3] or implicit representation of domain through the notion of location of a program [4]. We focus here on the implicit approach because it allows us to maintain a flat structure of boxes still describing compartments [11]. Flat structures are more efficient to implement simulators. We only need to associate every box with a location. Then all the boxes in the same

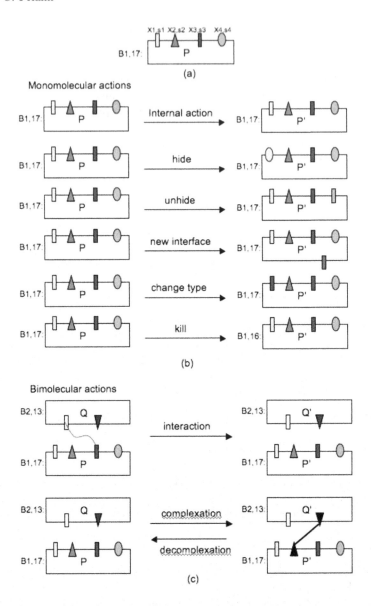

Fig. 6. Boxes, monomolecular and bimolecular operations. (a) Representation of a biological entity named B1 of 17 copies are available. The internal program P drives the behavior of the entity and the interfaces specify the interaction capabilities. Rectangle interfaces are active sites, triangle interfaces are complexed interfaces and oval represents hidden sites. The color of the sites denotes their type or interaction affinity. (b) The set of available monomolecular actions. The first one is just an internal updating that affect the P program. The other actions are needed to manipulate interfaces. Note that the kill action affects the number of available copies of the entity. (c) Bimolecular actions model exchange of information (the first action) or creation and destruction of complexes (the last two actions).

location are interpreted as being in the same compartment. Hierarchy of compartments is then obtained by imposing a containment relation over locations. A practical solutions is to use a tree-structure imposed by indexes similar to the ones of Dewey. For instance, consider the system represented in Fig. 5. The box b_i is represented by $024, b_i$ or the box b_j by $03, b_j$, where locations are paths in the hierarchy. Furthermore, the the fact that b_1 and b_2 are in the same compartment is rendered by using the same location 01 for both b_1 and b_2. Summing up, process calculi are suitable to represent compartments as well.

4   Potentials

The perspectives that emerge from the biological modeling based on process calculi are both in the life science domain and in the computer science domain. As far as life science is concerned, the predictive power of the approach could be exploited to inform wet biologists and help them planning focused experiments. An application is the description of a systems and then the study of its behavior under predefined perturbations. A perturbation in our approach is simply the adding of a new program to the set of the ones defining the system and inspecting the results of the new execution of the model. Clearly this capability is of interest both in better understanding the aetiology of diseases and in the definition of new drugs that exactly act on the causes of diseases. Note that the perturbation of a system can be caused by environmental factors in the case of diseases or by drugs when we want to inspect whether a molecule can stop or even prevent a disease. Furthermore, we can also think of perturbation caused by molecules contained in foods to test their toxicity or their actions on some diseases (for instance nutrigenomics could benefit from this approach).

Biology is mainly driven by quantities that emerge from real experiments. Hence we need to connect wet experiments and models in such a way that the available knowledge is used to inform simulators and hence constrain their levels of freedom. The iteration of these action should lead to an exact model of the phenomenon considered. To address this issue the bayesian inference of rate parameters from measures of concentrations at different times seems to be a promising approach.

Since process calculi are linguistic constructs to describe the dynamics of systems, they could heavily influence the definition of exchange model formalisms like SBML [8]. In fact, one of the main limitation of xml-based approaches is the inherent ambiguity of the descriptions that makes it hard to develop automatic translators into formal tools for analysing and simulating systems. Process calculi based notation could integrate SBML-like description languages to limit ambiguity and hence improve the already valuable usefulness of SBML. Of course, adding a degree of dynamics to static xml-based descriptions could be of interest also for computer science applications.

The real challenge we face in modeling biological systems is the definition of artificial systems that resemble the real biological behavior at a level of details that allows us to use them in place of animal models of diseases. This goal is still far from being available, but we need to work in that direction by addressing real biology and by letting us driven by biology if we want our community to grow and to be beneficial for life scientists.

The impact of the proposed approach on computer science can be further explained in terms of medium and long term goal. The medium term goal is the development of a set of quantitative tools for the modeling and analysis of complex artificial systems like sensor networks or hybrid large networks. Performance prediction, load balancing and pricing are all issues that deserve quantitative frameworks that share the incremental properties we showed for the βWB.

Another huge applicative domain that could benefit of the outcome of biological modeling is the one of web-services. In fact, orchestration and contract negotiation is an interaction which is inherently not key-lock. Hence understanding how biological interaction is driven and modeled could provide breakthrough insights on the definition and implementation of new and better web-services.

Long term goals concern the definition of new computational models and new programming languages that allow us to build software systems that are more robust, fault tolerant, secure than the current ones. All the mentioned properties are typical of biological systems, but are lacking in the actual artifacts. If we can enhance our understanding of biological functioning, we could get inspiration for a new generation of software developing environments.

5 Conclusions

The new field of computational and systems biology can have a large impact on the future of science and society. The engine driving the new coming discipline is its inherent interdisciplinarity at the convergence of computer science and life sciences. To continue fueling the progress of the field we must ensure a peer-to-peer collaboration between the scientists of the two disciplines. In fact if one discipline is considered a service for the other the cross-fertilization will stop soon. We must create common expectations and really joint projects in which both computer science and biology can enhance their state-of-the-art.

We must ensure a critical mass of people working in the field and a common language to exchange ideas. This is a major problem in current collaborations due to the lack of curricula that form people to work in this intersection area. We must invest time and resources in creating interdisciplinary curricula (together with new ways of recruiting people considering interdisciplinarity an added value) to form the new researchers of tomorrow.

Summing up, although a lot has still to be done, we started a new way of making science that can lead in the next years to unravel the machinery of cell behavior that in turn can lead to the creation of artificial systems enjoying the properties of living systems. Computational thinking is different way of approaching a problem by producing descriptions that are inherently executable (differently, e.g., from a set of equation). Furthermore the same specification can be examined at different level of abstractions simply by building a virtual hierarchy of interpretations. This a common practice in computer science where artificial systems are usually defined and described in layers depending on the growing abstraction from the physical architecture.

Acknowledgements. I would like to thank the whole research and admin team of CoSBi for the fruitful discussions and the beautiful environment in which it is my pleasure to work. I would like to thank Stephen Emmott and Luca Cardelli as well.

References

1. Calder, M., Gilmore, S., Hillston, J.: Modelling the influence of RKIP on the ERK signalling pathway using the stochastic process algebra PEPA. In: Dumke, R.R., Abran, A. (eds.) IWSM 2000. LNCS, vol. 4230, Springer, Heidelberg (2006)
2. Danos, V., Schachter, V. (eds.): CMSB 2004. LNCS (LNBI), vol. 3082. Springer, Heidelberg (2005)
3. Cardelli, L., Gordon, A.D.: Mobile ambients. In: Nivat, M. (ed.) ETAPS 1998 and FOSSACS 1998. LNCS, vol. 1378, Springer, Heidelberg (1998)
4. Castellani, I.: Process algebras with localities. In: Bergstra, J., Ponse, A., Smolka, S. (eds.) Handbook of Process Algebra, pp. 945–1046 (2001)
5. Ciobanu, G., Rozenberg, G. (eds.): Modelling in Molecular Biology. Springer, Heidelberg (2004)
6. Danos, V., Krivine, J.: Formal Molecular Biology done in CCS-R. In: Proceedings of Workshop on Concurrent Models in Molecular Biology (Bio-CONCUR'03). Electronic Notes in Theoretical Computer Science (2003)
7. Danos, V., Laneve, C.: Formal molecular biology. TCS 325(1) (2004)
8. Finney, A., Sauro, H., Hucka, M., Bolouri, H.: An xml-based model description language for systems biology simulations. Technical report, California Institute of Technology, Technical report (September 2000)
9. Gillespie, D.T.: Exact stochastic simulation of coupled chemical reactions. Journal of Physical Chemistry 81(25), 2340–2361 (1977)
10. Goss, P.J.E., Peccoud, J.: Quantitative modeling of stochastic systems in molecular biology by using stochastic Petri nets. In: Proceedings of the National Academy of Sciences, USA, vol. 12, pp. 6750–6754 (1998)
11. Guerriero, M.L., Priami, C., Romanel, A.: Beta-binders with static compartments. In: Algebraic Biology, 2007. to appear. Also TR-09-2006. The Microsoft Research - University of Trento Centre for Computational and Systems Biology (2007)
12. Hoare, C.A.R.: Communicating sequential processes. Communications of the ACM 21(8), 666–677 (1978)
13. Hood, L., Galas, D.: The digital code of DNA. Nature 421, 444–448 (2003)
14. Kuttler, C., Niehren, J.: Gene regulation in the pi-calculus: simulating cooperativity at the lambda switch. In: Priami, C., Ingólfsdóttir, A., Mishra, B., Nielson, H.R. (eds.) Transactions on Computational Systems Biology VII. LNCS (LNBI), vol. 4230, Springer, Heidelberg (2006)
15. Milner, R.: Communication and Concurrency. International Series in Computer Science. Prentice-Hall, Englewood Cliffs (1989)
16. Milner, R.: Communicating and mobile systems: the π-calculus. Cambridge Universtity Press, Cambridge (1999)
17. Palsson, B.O.: Systems Biology. Properties of reconstructed networks. Cambridge Universtity Press, Cambridge (2006)

18. Păun, G. (ed.): Membrane Computing. An Introduction. Springer, Heidelberg (2002)
19. Phillips, A., Cardelli, L.: A Correct Abstract Machine for the Stochastic Pi-calculus. In: Priami, C., Ingólfsdóttir, A., Mishra, B., Nielson, H.R. (eds.) Transactions on Computational Systems Biology VII. LNCS (LNBI), vol. 4230, Springer, Heidelberg (2006)
20. Priami, C.: Stochastic π-calculus. The Computer Journal 38(6), 578–589 (1995)
21. Priami, C., Quaglia, P.: Beta Binders for Biological Interactions. In: Danos, V., Schachter, V. (eds.) CMSB 2004. LNCS (LNBI), vol. 3082, pp. 20–33. Springer, Heidelberg (2005)
22. Priami, C., Regev, A., Silverman, W., Shapiro, E.: Application of a stochastic name-passing calculus to representation and simulation of molecular processes. Information Processing Letters 80(1), 25–31 (2001)
23. Regev, A., Panina, E.M., Silverman, W., Cardelli, L., Shapiro, E.: BioAmbients: An Abstraction for Biological Compartments. TCS 325(1) (2004)
24. Regev, A., Shapiro, E.: Cells as computation. Nature 419(6905), 343 (2002)
25. Romanel, A., Dematté, L., Priami, C.: The Beta Workbench. Technical Report TR-3-2007, The Microsoft Research - University of Trento Centre for Computational and Systems Biology (February 2007)
26. Wing, J.: Computational thinking. Communications of the ACM 49(3), 33–35 (2006)

End-to-End Information Management for Systems Biology

Peter Saffrey, Ofer Margoninski, James Hetherington,
Marta Varela-Rey, Sachie Yamaji, Anthony Finkelstein,
David Bogle, and Anne Warner

Centre for Mathematics and Physics in the Life and Experimental Sciences
(CoMPLEX), University College London (UCL), Gower Street, London

Abstract. Mathematical and computational modelling are research areas with increasing importance in the study of behaviour in complex biological systems. With the increasing breadth and depth of models under consideration, a disciplined approach to managing the diverse data associated with these models is needed. Of particular importance is the issue of provenance, where a model result is linked to information about the generating model, the parameters used in that model and the papers and experiments that were used to derive those parameters. This paper presents an architecture to manage this information along with accompanying tool support and examples of the management system in use at various points in the development of a large model.

1 Introduction

Recent years have seen the proliferation of computational and mathematical modelling for studying the behaviour of complex biological systems. Biological models have grown from the small scale and specific, such as [12] (squid axon) to whole organ models as described in [17] (Noble/Hunter heart model). The emerging discipline of Systems Biology deals with the latter category, where models of small aspects of physiology are used in synergy to bring a system level understanding.

As the scale of modelling projects grows, it becomes increasingly difficult to keep track of information pertaining to the models being used. Such information includes not only primary data, such as the encoding of a model or the resulting time course of a variable, but also *meta-data* that provides extra detail about the construction, origin and use of the primary data. It should be possible to trace the analysis of a model from end-to-end: from a modelling result to a model and the modelling decisions on which it was based and from there to experimental and literature sources for those decisions. This information trail needs to be continually reviewed and updated by experimentalists and modellers alike to support and justify results and to maximise reuse of previous research.

To achieve these goals a complete information management architecture for Systems Biology is needed. This architecture should capture data from all the distributed work areas of a multi-disciplinary project and allow data to be searched

C. Priami (Ed.): Trans. on Comput. Syst. Biol. VIII, LNBI 4780, pp. 77–91, 2007.

and amended as necessary. Stored information should integrate directly into modelling tools. Output from models should also be made available along with the supporting information used to produce those results.

In this paper we present such an architecture. The overall aims of the architecture are:

End-to-end management. Integrate data from every stage in the modelling process.

Separation of data and meta-data. By clearly separating model meta-data from model definitions, experimental data and other supporting information we can permit the management of model meta-data while allowing existing model and result storage formats to be used unchanged. This results in a framework which is 'light-weight' in the sense that it can be adopted with a minimum of changes to existing patterns of work.

Separation of modelling issues. Data about models, parameters and papers should be stored separately to enable easier re-use.

Modelling tool compatibility. Do not lock users to a particular modelling or analysis tool, but provide facilities to integrate stored data with a variety of tools.

Automation. Integrate our tools directly with modelling tools to automate model alteration, execution and storage tasks.

Distributed access. Provide access to all the facilities of the architecture, including model execution, through a standardised web-interface. This eases the capture of information from biologists and modellers alike.

In [6] we provided a biological meta-model, a high level view of biological modelling and how it can be organised. The present paper describes a *service based architecture* to manage the various information used in biological modelling, presenting a multi-component model of Glucose Homeostasis in human hepatocytes as a case study.

Although this paper is concerned with biological modelling, we do not address in detail any specific biological or modelling results. The outcomes presented pertain to more efficient and effective modelling in general, rather than any model or models in particular. We address the methodology of building large scale biological models by applying modern computer science techniques to Systems Biology, rather than deliberately advancing computer science itself.

2   Related Work

2.1   Data Management

Databases are available to manage several areas related to Systems Biology. Bibliographic databases such as Endnote are in common use. Similarly, laboratory information management systems (LIMS) such as ConturELN, Water eLab Notebook and DOE2000 are widely used for capturing and managing experimental information.

These tools are a useful part of modern research methods. However, they contain many features that clutter an end-to-end modelling driven approach. LIMS systems, for example, emphasise the process and consumable maintenance aspects of experimental work which are of little interest to modellers.

Our framework emphasises light-weight, simple tools that are integrated to capture and link information specific to modelling. The modular nature of our work means that future development of the architecture could connect directly to the databases used by LIMS and bibliographic systems, to make existing data repositories available in a modelling context.

2.2   Software Engineering Tools

Modelling for biology has features in common with traditional software engineering. Models are often software artefacts that evolve through a number of different versions. Models can be based on the work of teams of distributed researchers, like software, and communication and a shared understanding between these collaborators is vital to success. Software, like models, usually connects to configuration information (parameters) that need to be carefully tracked and managed.

There are a variety of tools for helping manage information pertaining to software projects. These vary from simple version control systems like CVS [5] and Bitkeeper [10] up to more sophisticated CASE tools [7].

Despite their superficial similarities, there are some fundamental differences between software engineering and biological modelling. The root of these differences is that modelling is an exploratory (divergent) discipline, where the only fixed goal is that of increased understanding, whereas software engineering is designed to converge on a single working solution to a known problem. This results in a number of differences between the two disciplines.

Version control. In software a new version almost always represents an improved version either with more features or with errors removed. In modelling, a new version may represent a test of a modelling hypothesis, which does not necessarily represent an improvement on an old model. Several parts of the model may be subject to this hypothesis testing.

For example, a pathway model may be based on two signalling cascades A and B, each of which includes a number of reactions. The choice of reactions to model can have several versions in both cascades, giving rise to versions A1, A2 and A3 for one cascade and B1, B2 and B3 for the other. It may be useful to test combinations of these, such as A1 with B3 and A3 with B2, particularly if these combinations of reactions enable different types of cross talk between the cascades. This combinatorial testing is very rarely needed in software and is therefore difficult to achieve with software version systems.

Configuration management. Software configuration is designed to be kept consistent and to avoid contradictions. Biological information used in model configurations, such as model parameter data, is not only constantly changing but there can be many conflicting theories about the same part of the system at one time.

Multi-disciplinary teams. Software development tools are designed for users who are highly computer literate. Modelling projects have diverse multi-disciplinary contributors, many of whom can benefit from access to modelling software even when they are not proficient in these types of tools. Modelling tools should address the accessibility and usability concerns raised by these diverse teams.

2.3   Collaboration Tools

There are other distributed collaboration environments designed to manage and share information. Examples include wiki-based systems such as Wikipedia [21] and more structured working environments like BSCW [4].

These systems can be very powerful when applied in the right environment. However, they are generic solutions and are not specifically designed to tackle the problems of biological modelling. Generic solutions can capture all the necessary data but their open-ended nature make tool support and integration with other software much more difficult. Our system constrains the type of data stored in order to maximise automation, allowing relevant information to interface with a variety of tools and presentations. Examples of this can be seen in section 5.4, where we interface parameter information and model results with common modelling and visualisation tools.

2.4   Model Repositories

Repositories of modelling information are becoming increasingly common. The biomodels.net project [18] is a repository of models based on the Systems Biology Markup Language (SBML) [13], a standard language for representing models of biochemical reaction networks.

To increase the accessibility of such models, an annotation standard has been proposed, the Minimal Information Requested In the Annotation of biochemical Models (MIRIAM) [19]. The standard is at an early stage, but aims to augment the SBML descriptions of models with meta-data providing provenance information, including links to existing databases.

Our work addresses the concerns raised by the MIRIAM standard. We provide tools to apply extensive meta-data descriptions of all parts of a model, including author and provenance information. Model meta-data can be linked to existing repositories of biological information. We take this one stage further by addressing model results. We differ from MIRIAM in that we separate model meta-data from the model itself, to facilitate the reuse of data in separate models.

We do not specify what modelling technology is used to implement the models themselves, and our architecture would allow SBML models to be linked to model meta-data and executed using one of the existing SBML model integration tools.

3   Architecture Description

Figure 1 shows an overview of our service architecture, presented as a UML2 component diagram. The key features of the architecture are as follows:

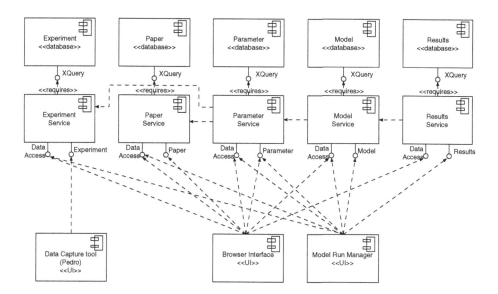

Fig. 1. Service based architecture overview

- Each specific area of modelling is managed by a *service*, which includes a database and a variety of tools to present and manage this information as well as connect it to other services. Services are implemented as Web Services, exposing their functionality via XML-RPC [20]. The tools described in this paper are built on top of these services. Using a standardised access method like XML-RPC makes it easier for third party tools to gain access to the facilities provided by each service.
- Our architecture manages only the meta-data about each element of biological modelling, providing links to the data itself. Thus, entries in the paper service can contain references into Pub-Med [1] and other bibliographic databases, parameter entries can contain references to relevant ontologies such as the gene ontology [3] and other data sources while model entries point to the model files that implement each model. Our services provide the necessary information to make modelling decisions and links as the means to obtain more detailed information, as necessary.
- Data about one model can be spread across several services, including paper, experiment and parameter information, rather than embedding this information into the description of the model itself. This means the parameters and the supporting information are independent of the model and can be referenced and reused by subsequent models.

– Data in the architecture is stored as XML in the native XML database
  eXist [16]. Where possible we have used existing XML languages such as
  BIBTEXML [9] and the Composite Model Description Language (CMDL)
  [15]. Using XML allows us to make use of the wealth of tool support for XML
  data, making it easier to present this information through a web browser,
  query stored data and integrate this information with modelling tools.

A possible use-case for the architecture is as follows:

1. Experimental work takes place and results are uploaded to the experiment
   service.
2. Literature pertinent to the model and experiments under consideration is
   studied and relevant papers uploaded to the paper service.
3. Using information from the paper and experiment services, model design
   begins. The design requires a number of parameters which are uploaded to
   the parameter service. Other parameter values may be missing, and further
   experimentation and literature search may be necessary.
4. A complete version of the model is uploaded into the model service.
5. This model is executed a number of times, generating a number of results.
   During this process, further possible values for each parameter are added to
   the parameter service, along with justifying information. These new values co-
   exist with the initial ideas for these parameters, as described in section 5.2.
6. These results are analysed, motivating further experimentation and the development of further models.

4   Tool Support

The service architecture is supported by a number of software tools for uploading,
browsing and applying stored data. Web-based tools provide distributed access
to the various services. The Model Run Manager brings together all the services
and demonstrates the full end-to-end potential of the architecture. There are
also more isolated tools to attend individual services.

4.1   Web Tools

To increase accessibility, several of the services have been exposed on our project
web page. The paper, experiment and parameter services can all be searched online and paper information can also be uploaded. In addition, the web page access
to the parameter service allows new values to be added to existing parameters,
new paper or experiment origins added to values and notes on parameters to be
edited.

Figure 2 shows a parameter under display via the web tool. Links provide
access to justifying papers for each value. The various buttons allow other users
to edit notes, add values to this parameter or add a justifying origin for an
existing value.

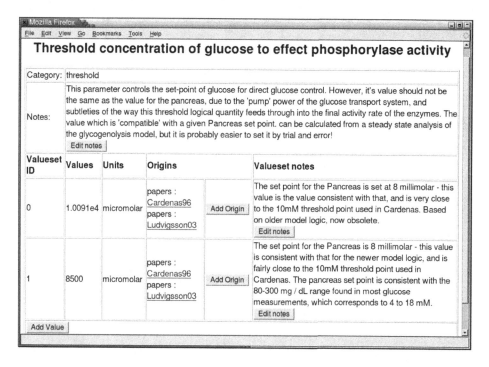

Fig. 2. Parameter display web tool screenshot

4.2   Model Run Manager

The Model Run Manager (MRM) is a graphical tool, designed to wrap the various services and integrate this data through model execution. MRM offers the following features:

- Read model descriptions and display information about parameters and inputs to those models, along with any visualisations of the model.
- Display and update information about parameters and parameter references in the parameter service and linked services.
- Perform model executions based on chosen parameter values and inputs, invoking the underlying model execution engine (such as Mathematica) without further intervention from the user.
- Generate web-based model reports based on each model execution, described in the next section.

Each of these tasks takes place in communication with the relevant services, so that all MRM users are accessing and updating the same data.

We have implemented MRM both as a standalone application and as a web page. The standalone application is designed for use by modellers to prepare a model for use on the web application.

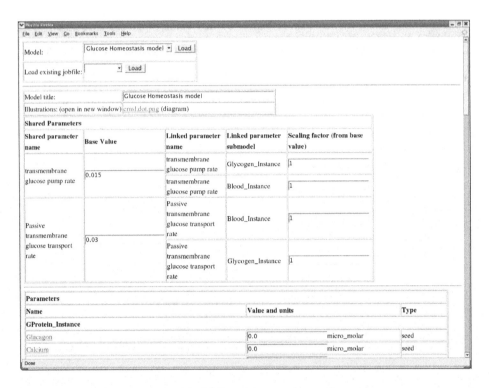

Fig. 3. Model Run Manager screenshot

Figure 3 shows a screenshot of the web version of MRM in use on a glucose homeostasis model, which is described in greater detail in section 6. At the top of the screenshot are the selection boxes for the available models and the jobfiles for each model. Below this, the name of the model is displayed, and links to any illustrations for the model. Since this is a composite model, the next table lists parameters that are shared between several of the component models, including the scaling factor to this parameter in each model. This scaling factor is used to map between models that represent the same concept differently for example, one model may define one time unit to represent one second where another may represent one hour. Finally, the beginning of the listing of the parameters themselves, listed by the model in which they appear. Each parameter includes units and an entry box for the user to choose a value. Note that each model name is a link, which takes the user to the entry in the database for that parameter.

Model Reports. A model report is a key outcome of the architecture. The report displays model results, variable values with respect to time, model implementation information and the parameter values chosen for this run. Each parameter is linked to its entry in the database, so a user can immediately jump to a display that will allow them to browse for an alternative parameter value or comment on an existing value based on their findings. The report also includes links to the justifying entries, experiment or paper, for each parameter value chosen, so a user can quickly gain access to the primary data on which a value is based.

A model report is generated by parsing XML data from the various services, stored during a model run. This makes it easy to extend the software to filter this generation for different presentations. For example, we have implemented a filter that converts the data into a Matlab data file, so that the model run can be analysed using Matlab's sophisticated visualisation capabilities. These files can be made available for download with the model report so that analysis can be carried out by other members of the project team without running the model again.

Like the other services, reports are generated and exposed as public web pages, so they can be instantly communicated to project colleagues or printed out for reference.

4.3   Other Supporting Software

The experiment service must capture a diverse range of experiments and provide effective documentation for both modellers and experimentalists alike. For rapid prototyping purposes, we chose to implement this feature with an existing tool, rather than implement a web-based replacement.

To capture experimental information, we use Pedro [8], a data modelling tool from the University of Manchester. Pedro was originally built for use in the proteomics community, but has been designed to facilitate capture of generic information using XML schema. Pedro generates graphical entry forms from a minimum of configuration information. We have extended Pedro with plugins to contact the database and then deployed a copy of this software into the laboratory to allow experiments to be entered and uploaded.

Although the configuration for experimental data-capture is specific to our project, this configuration is quick and simple to adapt to different types of experimental data. It would also be easy to add further configuration to allow parameter and paper information to be captured, or to add additional services. The Pedro data entry could also co-exist with another entry method, such as a web-form. This flexibility is an important part of each service, to allow the architecture to be applied to a wide variety of modelling projects.

5   Implementation Details

5.1   Model Service

Models stored in the model service are encoded using the Composite Model Description Language (CMDL) [15]. For convenience, we provide an overview of the main features of CMDL.

CMDL was designed to describe models that are composite: constructed from a number of sub-models. However, CMDL is also useful to describe non-composite models since it provides details necessary to link a model with the various services provided by our architecture. CMDL descriptions are restricted to the meta-data associated with a model, leaving the detailed implementation of a model to a specific file format such as a Mathematica file. The details provided in a CMDL file include:

- What mathematical functionality this model provides; what kind of input it expects and what output it produces. For example, in the glucose homeostasis model, the input is a function describing a feeding regime and the output is a graph predicting blood glucose levels.
- The submodels used to construct this model and how they are connected together. Each submodel description is itself encoded as a distinct CMDL file. A model which cannot be decomposed into further submodels is referred to as an elementary model. In our architecture, links to submodels can be used to look up the component submodel descriptions in the model service.
- The parameters used by this model. Parameters specific to particular submodels are stored in these individual descriptions. Parameters that are common between models are represented at the higher level, along with any scaling between these parameters. Again, these parameter listings can be used to look up relevant parameter information in the parameter service.

In [15], we describe the *orchestrator*, a software tool for reading and executing composite models described in CMDL. Our architecture can manage the information used in an orchestrator run, but it can also be used for elementary models running in a supported environment. We currently support Mathematica and XPPAUT models. The interaction with these tools is described in section 5.4.

5.2 Parameter Service

The parameter service stores information about the numerical constants used for aspects of biology represented in models. The schema to store parameters is based on the following information:

- A long descriptive name for the parameter. This name is designed to be an unambiguous description of the parameter that can be used by other users to locate values for the same aspect of biology later.
- A category for this parameter, such as a rate constant.
- Some descriptive text about the purpose of this parameter
- A number of value sets, each of which includes:
  - A value or range of values.
  - Origins for this value set, such as from the literature or experiment.
  - Comments on this value set.

Since there is often contention about the proper value for a parameter, this schema allows the storage of multiple 'value sets' for each parameter. Each value set stores a set of values including whatever justifying evidence is available. Just as supporting information can contradict, so can the values stored in the various value sets. It is up to users of the parameter service to resolve this ambiguity by deciding which values are most appropriate for a particular model run.

The parameter service accumulates data about parameters that evolves as a project develops. Older discredited value sets cannot (and should not) be deleted because they represent an advance in understanding for which values are appropriate. Instead, comments can be added to say why these values are no longer believed to be correct. Future users can examine these comments and decide for themselves whether these values should be used or not.

5.3   Interpretation Service

The interpretation service stores the results of model executions. Each interpretation is stored with the following information:

- The model, input and parameter values for this run.
- File references to datafiles generated.
- A time stamp for the generation of this result.

An interpretation file captures all the information necessary to understand a model run so that analysis can be carried out at a later date without repeating that run. The interpretation service, via MRM, can also export this information as a Matlab file, as described in section 4.2 (model reports).

5.4   Model Execution

Each model execution is controlled by a jobfile, which brings together the data necessary to launch a model run. This includes:

- A link to the model itself, described as a CMDL file.
- A list of the parameters used by the model and values for those parameters.
- An input function for the model.

A jobfile stores a specific set of model settings, for example, parameter values that represent normal and pathological states of a biological system. Jobfiles are stored in a jobfile service where they can be accessed and reused by other users.

MRM uses information from each jobfile to prepare and execute the models. This includes uploading the chosen parameter values into the models. The architecture supports this parameter upload into Mathematica and XPPAUT models as well as composite models executed with the orchestrator. Composite models require subsets of the overall parameters to be uploaded into each sub-model, where some parameters may be shared between several sub-models.

Although parameters listed in jobfiles are linked to entries in the parameter service, the values are not dependent on these entries. If a value chosen in a jobfile has an entry in the parameter service, information from this entry is added to the model report, but values that have no entry can still be used. The architecture provides database support where desired, but does not disallow model runs where justifying information does not exist.

Once models have executed, MRM captures the output in the model report. By default, MRM presents image files generated by each model run, but it also contains native support for certain formats, such as those generated by the orchestrator, so that these can be rendered in a variety of graphical forms.

6   Case Study

To test the utility of the information management architecture, it has been used in a modelling task of some complexity. This section describes the model and presents a number of cases that occurred during its development and testing. We describe how these tasks were carried out with the support of the information management architecture and compare this with the same operations without such support.

In [11] we discussed an early version of the architecture in use for a much smaller version of the model presented here. The earlier version included only the parameter and an early version of the interpretation service, without the web exposure and report generation. This previous version can be thought of as testing individual services, whilst this paper addresses the integration of these services into a complete system.

6.1   Model Description

We are part of a research project at University College London whose aim is to produce a physiological model of the liver[2]. As part of the project, we have constructed a model describing glucose homeostasis[14]. Glucose is the readily available source of energy, which is being supplied by the blood to all cells in the body. Glucose is stored in the liver in the form of glycogen. Glycogen buildup and release in the liver is controlled by two hormones, Insulin and Glucagon, secreted by the Pancreas. Our model is able to predict glucose levels in the blood, as well as the time course of many other variables, as a function of the dietary regime and a set of parameters, such as the affinity of liver cells receptors to Insulin. Failure of glucose homeostasis is a key feature of diabetes. Detailed biological results from this model will appear in a future publication.

6.2   Composite Modelling

The glucose homeostasis model is a composite model, constructed by the assembly of a number of component models. The model currently has seven submodels, representing the glucagon activated G-Protein receptor, cyclic-AMP response, glycogen, insulin response, calcium response, the Pancreas and the Blood. The tools to specify and execute composite models, allowing the components to be of varying complexity and specified in different modelling environments, is described in [15].

A composite model provides a challenging test because there is a large amount of information to be managed. Each individual model is derived in isolation, but may share linked variables in composition. Models may also share parameters, some of which may require a scaling factor to be applied between models. Interesting model behaviour may be as a result of a very particular configuration of the various sub-components. Selecting a particular model configuration can be time-consuming and model execution itself may require specific knowledge of the model simulation tool in question; these are all areas in which our architecture aims to provide support and improve usability.

6.3   Modelling Use Cases

Deriving Parameters. Deriving parameters for models is a collaborative effort between modellers and experimentalists. Both groups must decide on what parameters are needed to represent the physiology in question and how best to apply these in a model.

In the early stages of development of the glucose homeostasis model, parameters were collated and exchanged using a spreadsheet, updated with face-to-face meetings. The information management architecture replaced this with a centralised resource where this information could be continually updated. A common issue was the clear description of the way in which a parameter was obtained by bringing together several values from the literature with a simple model. A structured presentation of these descriptions and the accessibility of an up-to-date information aided understanding of these parameters and how they are used. An example is the parameter for the rate of activity of the enzyme glycogen phosphorylase, which must be combined with data for enzyme concentrations and Michaelis constants if it is to be related to maximum activity rates found in enzyme databases.

Executing a Model on a Variety of Parameter Sets. Interesting model behaviour is often based on a particular set of parameter values and inputs. These values may represent a particular state of the biological system.

In the glucose homeostasis model, different sets of parameter values were used to represent different levels of diabetes, in our model represented by insulin resistance. These parameter sets could be quickly recalled so that models could be tested with different dietary regimes. Another example of this is the maintenance of three complete parameter sets for a calcium oscillations model, reflecting in-house and literature parameter searches, and a fit to data.

Model Results. Development of the glucose homeostasis model was sometimes hindered by a disconnect between modellers and experimentalists. Experimentalists did not always feel they understood the modelling process, including how models were used and what kind of results they could produce.

The MRM and model reports standardised the way in which our models accepted input and generated output. Where experimentalists could run models for themselves, and understand the results, they were more likely to feel part of the modelling process and able to contribute relevant data to it directly. One example benefit of this is the engagement of experimenters in the search for oscilliatory glucose phenomena. Such phenomena were first observed in the model, and a successful experimental programme is now ongoing. Similarly, modellers were able to improve model relevance by formulating model reports in a way that matched experimentalists expectations. This resulted in the construction of a model focussed on influence on Cyclic-AMP production by S-Adenosyl Methionine (SAM), a key supporting agent in the experimental system, but not initially of interest to modellers.

Parametric Model Errors. A model run may produce the wrong results because a parameter is incorrect or has been chosen from an inappropriate source.

In one example, our model produced output curves that were similar to the experimental results, but with time-scales on a different order of magnitude (highlighted by experimentalists observing model results). This problem was due to the glycogen phosphorylase activity parameter discussed above, a value for which had been obtained by in-vitro enzyme kinetic techniques conditions. The architecture made it simple to retrieve the relevant parameter set chosen and examine the justifying evidence to identify this problem. This could take place even as the model was being used to test a variety of other conditions, since the architecture automatically records each parameter set as it is executed, preventing any previous model configuration information from being lost.

Another benefit of the framework is managing potential conflict between parameters in a composite modelling setting. For example, a parameter representing the effective rate of glucose pumping into the cell due to the equilibrium between glucose and glucose-6-phosphate is shared between the glycogen and blood sub-models. Using the MRM means that this parameter only needs to be altered once, and this change automatically permuted to the two relevant sub-models. This is more convenient and intuitive than changing each model in turn, as well as less prone to human error.

7   Summary and Conclusions

We have presented an information management architecture for Systems Biology along with its accompanying tool support. We have described how our light-weight modular approach allows integration with existing tools and information reuse and how making the tools available through the web helps to capture and distribute information from a variety of disciplines. We have also presented our experiences from using the architecture in a large example.

Some of the case studies presented would still be possible with existing generic solutions. However, tools and databases designed specifically for modelling provided immediate benefits, such as automatic parameter upload and a stanardised user interface, that engaged users immediately and encouraged the more long term benefits, such as comprehensive provenance information on a particular model and data reuse.

Acknowledgements

This work was funded by a Beacon Project grant from the Department of Trade and Industry. We thank them for their support.

References

1. Pub med, http://www.ncbi.nlm.nih.gov/entrez/
2. The UCL Beacon Project, http://grid.ucl.ac.uk/biobeacon/

3. Ashburner, M., Ball, C.A., Blake, J.A., Botstein, D.: Gene ontology: tool for the unification of biology. Nat. Genet (2000)
4. Bentley, R., Horstmann, T., Sikkel, K., Trevor, J.: Collaborative information sharing with the World Wide Web: The BSCW shared workspace system. In: Proceedings of the 4th International WWW Conference (1995)
5. Cederqvist, P.: Version management with cvs (2002)
6. Finkelstein, A., Hetherington, J., Li, L., Margoninski, O., Saffrey, P., Seymour, R., Warner, A.: Computational challenges of systems biology. IEEE Computer 37(5), 26–33 (2004)
7. Fisher, A.S.: CASE: using software development tools (1988)
8. Garwood, K.L., Taylor, C.F., Runte, K.J., Brass, A., Oliver, S.G., Paton, N.W.: Pedro: a configurable data entry tool for XML. Bioinformatics (2004)
9. Hendrikse, Z.: An XML equivalent of BibTeX: bibteXML. Available at xml: coverpages: org= bibteXML: html (June 2001)
10. Henson, V., Garzik, J.: Bitkeeper for kernel developers. Ottawa Linux Symposium (2002) Address: http://www.linux.org.uk/
11. Hetherington, J., Bogle, I.D.L., Saffrey, P., Margoninski, O., Li, L., Yamaji, S., Finkelstein, A., Callard, R., Seymour, R., Horton, R., Warner, A.: Addressing the challenges of multiscale model management in systems biology (accepted for publication) Computers and Chemical Engineering (2006)
12. Hodgkin, A.L., Katz, B.: The effect of sodium ions on the electrical activity of the giant axon of the squid. J. Physiol., Lond (1949)
13. Hucka, M., Finney, A., Sauro, H.M., Bolouri, H., Doyle, J.C.: The systems biology markup language (SBML): a medium for representation and exchange of biochemical models. Bioinformatics (2003)
14. Klover, P.J., Mooney, R.A.: Hepatocytes: critical for glucose homeostasis. Int J Biochem Cell Biol 36(5), 753–758 (2004)
15. Margoninski, O., Saffrey, P., Hetherington, J., Finkelstein, A., Warner, A.: A specification language and a framework for the execution of composite models in systems biology (in press) Transactions of Computational Systems Biology (2006)
16. Meier, W.: eXist: An open source native XML database. Web, Web-Services, and Database Systems (2002)
17. Noble, D.: Modeling the heart–from genes to cells to the whole organ. Science (2002)
18. Le Novère, N., Bornstein, B., Broicher, A., Courtot, M.: Biomodels database: a free, centralized database of curated, published, quantitative kinetic models. Nucleic Acids Res (2006)
19. Le Novère, N., Finney, A., Hucka, M., Bhalla, U.: Minimum information requested in the annotation of biochemical models (MIRIAM). Nature Biotechnology 23, 1509–1515 (2005)
20. StLaurent, S., Johnston, J., Dumbill, E.: Programming web services with XML-RPC. IBM System Journal (2001)
21. Wikipedia, U.O.: Wikipedia-the free encyclopedia. wikipedia homepage, 2006 (2006)

On Differentiation and Homeostatic Behaviours of Boolean Dynamical Systems[*]

Élisabeth Remy and Paul Ruet

CNRS - Institut de Mathématiques de Luminy,
163 avenue de Luminy, Case 907, 13288 Marseille Cedex 9 France
{remy,ruet}@iml.univ-mrs.fr

Abstract. We study rules proposed by the biologist R. Thomas relating the structure of a concurrent system of interacting genes (represented by a signed directed graph called a regulatory graph) with its dynamical properties. We prove that the results in [10] are stable under projection, and this enables us to relax the assumptions under which they are valid. More precisely, we relate here the presence of a positive (resp. negative) circuit in a regulatory graph to a more general form of biological differentiation (resp. of homeostasis).

1 Introduction

The activity of a biological cell is to a large extent controlled by genetic regulation, which is an interacting process involving proteins and DNA (genes). We are interested here in genetic regulatory networks which abstract from the detailed genome-protein interaction by focussing on the genome and by considering interactions between genes. Such a simplification is somehow justified by the importance of DNA as a program which is present in all the cells of an organism (whereas the concentrations in proteins and in RNA transcribed from DNA vary according to the cell and the time). Genetic regulatory networks have the structure of a signed directed graph, where vertices represent genes and directed edges come equipped with a sign (+1 or −1) and represent activatory or inhibitory effect.

This paper deals with properties relating the structure of such a concurrent system of interacting genes with its dynamics. We shall consider here discretised Boolean dynamics,[1] where the activity of a gene in a specific cell is measured by the concentration of the RNA transcripted from DNA, a quantity called the

---

[*] Corrected version of the paper published in the Transactions on Computational Systems Biology VII, Springer LNCS 4230: 153-162, 2006.

[1] Discrete approaches are increasingly used in biology because of the qualitative nature of most experimental data, together with a wide occurrence of non-linear regulatory relationships (e.g., combinatorial arrangements of molecular bindings, existence of cooperative or antagonist regulatory effects).

C. Priami (Ed.): Trans. on Comput. Syst. Biol. VIII, LNBI 4780, pp. 92–101, 2007.
© Springer-Verlag Berlin Heidelberg 2007

expression level of the gene and assumed to be either 1 (gene expressed) or 0 (gene not expressed). Hence the state of a system of n genes is modelled by an n-tuple $x \in \{0,1\}^n$. The concurrent nature of these biological objects is clearly demonstrated for instance by a mapping to standard Petri nets [2,9], of which genetic regulatory graphs can be considered as a subsystem.

The starting point of this work consists in two simple rules stated by the biologist R. Thomas and relating the structure of regulatory graphs to their asymptotic dynamical properties [17]:

1. a necessary condition for multistability (i.e., the existence of several stable fixed points in the dynamics) is the existence of a positive circuit in the regulatory graph (the sign of a circuit being the product of the signs of its edges): this corresponds to cell differentiation processes;
2. a necessary condition for the existence of an attractive cycle in the dynamics is the existence of a negative circuit: this corresponds to homeostasis (sustained oscillatory behaviours, e.g., cell cycle or circadian rhythms).

These rules have given rise to mathematical statements and proofs mostly in a differential dynamical formalism [8,14,4,15], and more recently in the discrete Boolean formalism [1,10]. By proving in this paper that these properties are stable under projection (in a sense that we make precise in Lemma 1), we generalise the results in [10] by showing that the existence of positive and negative circuits actually follows from weaker assumptions (Theorems 3 and 4). In the case of positive circuits for instance, the condition corresponds to a more general form of differentiation than in [10].

We do not make explicit in this introduction how regulatory graphs and dynamics are defined in terms of each other. This is done in Section 2. Let us simply observe here that instead of starting from processes which are graphs and studying their dynamics (which is typically graph rewriting, see [3] in the case of protein-protein interaction), we start here with a given dynamics and derive a regulatory graph at each point of the phase space (via a discrete form of Jacobian matrix). In particular, our approach can be used to infer circuits in regulatory networks. It is also possible to consider a fixed global "topology" of interacting genes, e.g., by taking the union of the graphs over points in the phase space, and to view our local graphs as annotations of the global one (where an interaction is "active" in a certain region of the phase space). Observe however that these more global graphs need not immediately correspond to the usual interaction graphs considered by biologists: for instance, as noticed in [16], the positive circuits occurring in [5,7] are not regulatory feedback circuits, and the regulatory graphs defined in [6] are the same as ours only up to self-regulations.

We believe that the kind of properties at hand in this paper should serve as a basis to study more refined models, which could in particular take into account stochastic phenomena and metabolic pathways.

2   Thomas' Rules and Stability Under Projection

2.1   Preliminaries

We start by recalling here the definitions which enable to associate regulatory graphs to a dynamics. The paper is self-contained, though more details can be found in [10].

Let n be a positive integer. The integers $1, \dots, n$ denote genes. A *state* of the system is an $x = (x_1, \dots, x_n) \in \{0,1\}^n$, where x_i is the (discretised) expression level of gene i: $x_i = 1$ when gene i is expressed, 0 otherwise. For $\beta \in \{0,1\}$, we define $\bar{\beta}$ by $\bar{0} = 1$ and $\bar{1} = 0$. For $x \in \{0,1\}^n$ and $I \subseteq \{1, \dots, n\}$, $\bar{x}^I \in \{0,1\}^n$ is defined by $(\bar{x}^I)_i = x_i$ for $i \notin I$ and $(\bar{x}^I)_i = \bar{x_i}$ for $i \in I$. When $I = \{i\}$ is a singleton, $\bar{x}^{\{i\}}$ is denoted by $\bar{x}^i$.

Dynamics. We are interested in the dynamics of the system consisting in the n interacting genes. Consider a map $f : \{0,1\}^n \to \{0,1\}^n$, $f(x) = (f_1(x), \dots, f_n(x))$. For each $x \in \{0,1\}^n$ and $i = 1, \dots, n$, $f_i(x)$ denotes the value to which x_i, the expression level of gene i, tends when the system is in state x. We assume that the system evolves according to the (non-deterministic) *asynchronous dynamics* $\{(x, \bar{x}^i) \text{ s.t. } x \in \{0,1\}^n, x_i \neq f_i(x)\}$, i.e., the expression level of only one gene is updated at each step. Other dynamics can be considered, like the (deterministic) synchronous dynamics $\{(x, f(x)) \text{ s.t. } x \in \{0,1\}^n\}$ where all the expression levels x_i are simultaneously updated to $f_i(x)$ in one step. But as argued in [10], the asynchronous one is more realistic, and Theorem 2 for instance does not hold for the synchronous one. Observe that kinetic parameters are not taken into account in the discrete approach considered in this paper; however the model could be enriched by temporal delays: this would enable to recover kinetic informations.

A *cycle (for f)* is a sequence of states $(x^1, \dots, x^r)$ such that for each $i = 1, \dots, r$, the pair (x^i, x^{i+1}) belongs to the (asynchronous) dynamics. Indices are taken here modulo r, i.e., $r + 1 = 1$. A cycle $(x^1, \dots, x^r)$ is completely described by one of its points, say x^1, and its *strategy*, which is the map $\varphi : \{1, \dots, r\} \to \{1, \dots, n\}$ such that

$$x^{i+1} = \overline{x^i}^{\varphi(i)}.$$

A cycle $(x^1, \dots, x^r)$ with strategy φ is said to be a *trap cycle* when, once in the cycle, one cannot escape any more, i.e., for all $i = 1, \dots, r$:

$$f(x^i) = \overline{x^i}^{\varphi(i)}.$$

Regulatory Graphs. A *regulatory graph* is a signed directed graph with vertex set $\{1, \dots, n\}$, i.e., a directed graph with a sign, $+1$ or -1, attached to each edge. To $f : \{0,1\}^n \to \{0,1\}^n$ and $x \in \{0,1\}^n$, we associate a regulatory graph $G(f)(x)$ with an edge from j to i when

$$f_i(\bar{x}^j) \neq f_i(x),$$

with positive sign when

$$x_j = f_i(x),$$

and negative sign otherwise. The intuition for the first condition is straightforward, and actually the graph underlying $G(f)(x)$ (obtained by forgetting the signs) has adjacency matrix the *discrete Jacobian matrix* of f at x defined in [11,12] and recently used in [13] for proving a discrete version of Jacobian conjecture. The intuition for the second condition is that the edge is positive when the values x_j and $f_i(x)$ either both increase or both decrease.

If $I \subseteq \{1, \dots, n\}$, an *I-circuit* is a circuit $(n_1, \dots, n_k)$ such that $n_1, \dots, n_k \in I$. If $J \subseteq I$, a *J*-circuit is clearly an *I*-circuit. The *sign of a circuit* is the product of the signs of its edges.

If G is a regulatory graph and $I \subseteq \{1, \dots, n\}$, the *restriction of G to I* is the regulatory graph obtained from G by removing any vertex not in I and any edge whose source or target is not in I.

Thomas' Rules. The following results have been proved in [10].

Theorem 1. *Let $f : \{0,1\}^n \to \{0,1\}^n$. If f has at least two fixed points, then there is an $x \in \{0,1\}^n$ such that $G(f)(x)$ has a positive circuit. More precisely, if f has two fixed points a and b, and if I is such that $b = \bar{a}^I$, then there is an $x \in \{0,1\}^n$ such that $G(f)(x)$ has a positive I-circuit.*

Theorem 2. *If $f : \{0,1\}^n \to \{0,1\}^n$ has a trap cycle $(x^1, \dots, x^r)$ with strategy φ, then $G(f)(x^1) \cup \dots \cup G(f)(x^r)$ has a negative I-circuit with $I = \{\varphi(1), \dots, \varphi(r)\}$.*

Examples of biological situations illustrating these two kinds of dynamical properties have been studied for instance in [2]: drosophila cell cycle for an example of homeostasis and negative circuit, flowering of arabidopsis for an example of differentiation and positive circuit.

2.2   Stability Under Projection

We show that the regulatory graphs defined in Section 2.1 are stable under projection in the following sense.

Given $I \subseteq \{1, \dots, n\}$, let m be the cardinality of I, $m \leqslant n$, and let $\pi_I : \{0,1\}^n \to \{0,1\}^m$ be the projection on $\{0,1\}^m$. Given such a subset I of genes, there are several ways to define a dynamics on I: if $f : \{0,1\}^n \to \{0,1\}^n$ and $s : \{0,1\}^m \to \{0,1\}^n$ is a *section* of π_I (i.e., $\pi_I \circ s$ is the identity), let

$$f_{I,s} = \pi_I \circ f \circ s : \{0,1\}^m \to \{0,1\}^m.$$

We shall be especially interested in very specific sections, those for which genes out of I are given a fixed expression level: a section s is said *regular* when $\pi_k \circ s : \{0,1\}^m \to \{0,1\}$ is constant for each $k \notin I$.

Let us say furthermore that I is *compatible with f* when for all $x, y \in \{0,1\}^n$, $\pi_I(x) = \pi_I(y)$ implies $\pi_I(f(x)) = \pi_I(f(y))$. In that case, all the maps $f_{I,s}$, for

s a section of π_I, are equal, and we may let $f_I : \{0,1\}^m \to \{0,1\}^m$ be their common value: f_I is then also given by

$$f_I(z) = \pi_I(f(x))$$

for $x \in \{0,1\}^n$ any point *over* z, i.e., such that $\pi_I(x) = z$.

Lemma 1. *Let $f : \{0,1\}^n \to \{0,1\}^n$, $I \subseteq \{1,\ldots,n\}$ and $z \in \{0,1\}^m$. If s is a regular section of π_I, then $G(f_{I,s})(z)$ coincides with the restriction of $G(f)(s(z))$ to I. In particular, when I is compatible with f, $G(f_I)(z)$ is the restriction of $G(f)(x)$ to I for $x \in \{0,1\}^n$ any point over z.*

Proof — Let $i, j \in I$. The regulatory graph $G(f_{I,s})(z)$ contains an edge from j to i if, and only if,

$$(f_{I,s})_i(\bar{z}^j) \neq (f_{I,s})_i(z).$$

But $(f_{I,s})_i(z) = f_i(s(z))$ because

$$\pi_i \circ \pi_I = \pi_i$$

for $i \in I$. On the other hand, $(f_{I,s})_i(\bar{z}^j) = f_i\left(\overline{s(z)}^j\right)$ because, for $j \in I$, we have

$$s(\bar{z}^j) = \overline{s(z)}^j$$

since s is regular. Hence $G(f_{I,s})(z)$ has an edge from j to i if, and only if, $G(f)(s(z))$ has. The edge in $G(f_{I,s})(z)$ is positive if, and only if,

$$z_j = (f_{I,s})_i(z),$$

and the edge in $G(f)(s(z))$ is positive if, and only if,

$$s(z)_j = f_i(s(z)).$$

These conditions are equivalent for $i, j \in I$.   □

This Lemma asserts a sort of commutation property: the regulatory graph associated to the projected dynamics is the restriction of the initial regulatory graph. Observe however that the projection does not commute with the dynamics. Indeed, let us define the asynchronous dynamics of $f_{s,I}$: a pair $(z, z') \in \{0,1\}^m \times \{0,1\}^m$ with $z \neq z'$ is in the dynamics when there exists $x' \in \{0,1\}^n$ such that $z' = \pi_I(x')$ and $(s(z), x')$ belongs to the asynchronous dynamics of f. The point is that a pair (x, x') in the dynamics of f may satisfy $\pi_I(x) = \pi_I(x')$ (when $x' = \bar{x}^i$ with $i \notin I$) and hence not be mapped to a pair in the dynamics of $f_{s,I}$.

$$
\begin{array}{ccc}
x = s(z) & \cdots\cdots\!\!\!\longrightarrow & x' \\
s \uparrow & & \downarrow \pi_I \\
z & \longrightarrow & z'
\end{array}
$$

Observe that Lemma 1 does not hold when s is not regular. Let indeed f : $\{0,1\}^2 \to \{0,1\}^2$ be given by:

$$f(0,0) = (1,0)$$
$$f(1,0) = (1,1)$$
$$f(1,1) = (0,1)$$
$$f(0,1) = (0,0),$$

$I = \{1\}$ and $s(0) = (0,0), s(1) = (1,1)$: then $G(f_{I,s})(0)$ has a negative self-loop on 1 whereas $G(f)(s(0))$ consists in a positive edge from 1 to 2 and a negative edge from 2 to 1.

When I is compatible with f, the equivalence relation $\sim$ induced by the projection π_I between states ($x \sim y$ if, and only if, $\pi_I(x) = \pi_I(y)$) is a bisimulation for the asynchronous dynamics: indeed, it can be checked that if $x \sim y$ and (x, x') is in the dynamics of f, then there exists y' such that $x' \sim y'$ and (y, y') is in the dynamics of f.

Now, Lemma 1 enables us to relax the conditions of validity of Theorems 1 and 2, as we shall see in the following sections.

3   Disjoint Stable Subspaces and Positive Circuits

The process of biological differentiation does not necessarily correspond to multistationarity. Consider for instance the process which controls the lysis-lysogeny decision in the bacteriophage lambda. The dynamics has a single fixed point (lysogeny) and a trap cycle (lysis): these two stable subspaces can be viewed as a differentiation phenomenon, and we would like this to imply the existence of a positive circuit (which exists indeed in the regulatory graph associated to our example, between genes C1 and Cro). In this Section we show that holds in general for Boolean dynamics.

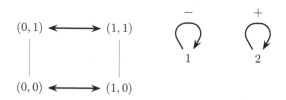

Fig. 1. On the left, a dynamics for $n = 2$ with no fixed point is pictured on a framed square, and a bold arrow from state x to state $\overline{x}^i$ means that $x_i \neq f_i(x)$. The x-axis carries the expression level of gene 1 and the y-axis the expression level of gene 2. On the right, a positive loop on gene 2 in the (constant) regulatory graph, in accordance with Theorem 3.

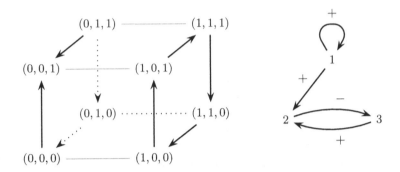

Fig. 2. On the left, a dynamics with a single fixed point $(0, 0, 1)$; dotted lines are only supposed to ease visualising the 3-cube. On the right, the regulatory graph associated to the state $(1, 1, 1)$ has a positive loop on 1, in accordance with Theorem 3.

Theorem 3. *Let $f : \{0, 1\}^n \to \{0, 1\}^n$, $I \subseteq \{1, \ldots, n\}$ and s a regular section of π_I. If $f_{I,s}$ has at least two fixed points, then there is an $x \in \{0, 1\}^n$ such that $G(f)(x)$ has a positive circuit. More precisely, if $f_{I,s}$ has two fixed points a and b, and if $J \subseteq I$ is such that $b = \bar{a}^J$, then there is an $x \in \{0, 1\}^n$ such that $G(f)(x)$ has a positive J-circuit.*

Proof — By Theorem 1, there is a $z \in \{0, 1\}^m$ such that $G(f_{I,s})(z)$ has a positive J-circuit, and Lemma 1 suffices to conclude. □

The following obvious Lemma states that multistationarity of f_I corresponds to the existence of disjoint subspaces which are stable under f, clearly a more general form of biological differentiation than multistationarity.

Lemma 2. *Let $f : \{0, 1\}^n \to \{0, 1\}^n$, $I \subseteq \{1, \ldots, n\}$ and $z \in \{0, 1\}^m$. When I is compatible with f, z is a fixed point for f_I if, and only if, the subspace $\pi_I^{-1}(z)$ is stable under f.*

For instance, the dynamics given in Figures 1 and 2 do not have multistability, but projecting the dynamics on the y-coordinate ($I = \{2\} \subseteq \{1, 2\}$ is compatible with f) in the first case and on the x-coordinate ($I = \{1\} \subseteq \{1, 2, 3\}$ is compatible with f, too) in the second case, gives rise to multistability and this explains in both cases the existence of a positive circuit in the regulatory graph associated to some state.

A possible generalisation of Theorem 3 would be that positive circuits are necessary for the genuine coexistence of disjoint attractors (in our framework: disjoint sets of states which are stable under the dynamics), a conjecture which still remains to be demonstrated.

It is worth observing that this stability under projection is independent from the framework. For instance, it may be applied to the differential framework in [15]. Indeed, let $\Omega \subseteq \mathbb{R}^n$ be a product of open intervals in $\mathbb{R}$ and $f : \Omega \to \mathbb{R}^n$.

The projection $p_I : \mathbb{R}^n \to \mathbb{R}^m$, where m is the cardinality of I, is given by

$$(p_I(x))_i = \begin{cases} x_i & \text{if } i \in I, \\ 0 & \text{otherwise,} \end{cases}$$

and compatibility of $I \subseteq \{1, \ldots, n\}$ with f is defined in the same way as in the Boolean case: for all $x, y \in \Omega$, $p_I(x) = p_I(y)$ implies $p_I(f(x)) = p_I(f(y))$. In that case, we may let $f_I : \mathbb{R}^m \to \mathbb{R}^m$ be defined by $f_I(z) = p_I(f(x))$ for $x \in \Omega$ any point over z. When f is continuously differentiable, C. Soulé associates to any $x \in \Omega$ a regulatory graph $G(f)(x)$ as follows: there is a positive (resp. negative) edge from j to i when the (i,j) entry $J(f)(x)_{i,j}$ of the Jacobian matrix is positive (resp. negative).

Now, when I is compatible with f, we have $(\partial(f_I)_i/\partial x_j)(z) = (\partial f_i/\partial x_j)(x)$ for x any point over z, hence the Jacobian matrix $J(f_I)(z)$ is a submatrix of $J(f)(x)$ and we get the following analogous of Lemma 1: if $x \in \Omega$ is any point over z, then $G(f_I)(z)$ is the restriction of $G(f)(x)$ to I. This implies the following slight generalisation of Theorem 1 in [15]: if $I \subseteq \{1, \ldots, n\}$ is compatible with f and f_I has at least two nondegenerate zeros (points a such that $f_I(a) = 0$ and $\det J(f_I)(a) \neq 0$), then there exists $x \in \Omega$ such that $G(f)(x)$ has a positive circuit.

4 Dynamic Cycles and Negative Circuits

Theorem 4. *Let $f : \{0,1\}^n \to \{0,1\}^n$, $I \subseteq \{1, \ldots, n\}$ and s a regular section of π_I. If $f_{I,s}$ has a trap cycle $(z^1, \ldots, z^r)$ with strategy φ, then*

$$G(f)(s(z^1)) \cup \cdots \cup G(f)(s(z^r))$$

has a negative J-circuit with $J = \{\varphi(1), \ldots, \varphi(r)\}$.

Proof — By Theorem 2, $G(f_{I,s})(z^1) \cup \cdots \cup G(f_{I,s})(z^r)$ has a negative circuit with vertices $\varphi(1), \ldots, \varphi(r)$. Since $\varphi(1), \ldots, \varphi(r) \in I$, by Lemma 1, this negative circuit is also in $G(f)(s(z^1)) \cup \cdots \cup G(f)(s(z^r))$. $\qquad\square$

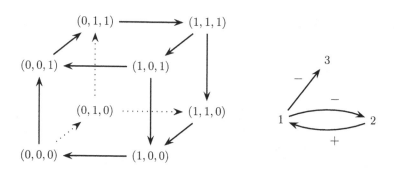

Fig. 3. On the left, a dynamics with no trap cycle. On the right, the regulatory graph associated to state $(0,0,0)$ has a negative circuit, in accordance with Theorem 4.

Figure 3 gives an example of dynamics with many dynamical cycles, none of which is a trap, hence Theorem 2 cannot be applied to infer some negative circuit. We observe that $I = \{1,2\} \subseteq \{1,2,3\}$ is compatible with f: the two horizontal cycles are in parallel planes. Then by projecting on I, we get a trap cycle, and this explains the negative circuit involving genes 1 and 2. In the present case, the negative circuit occurs in the regulatory graph $G(0,0,0)$ associated to a single state.

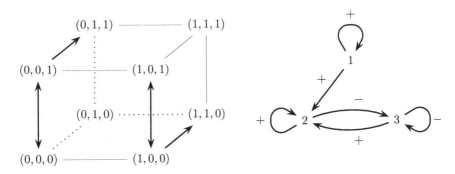

Fig. 4. On the left, a dynamics with both differentiation and homeostasis in different projections. On the right, the regulatory graph associated to state $(0,0,0)$.

A non trivial example of a dynamics with differentiation and homeostasis is given in Figure 4. On the one hand, projecting on $\{1\}$ is compatible with the dynamics and gives rise to multistationarity, whence a positive self-loop on 1. On the other hand, projecting on $\{3\}$ and taking the following regular section:

$$s(0) = (0,0,0)$$
$$s(1) = (0,0,1)$$

leads to a trap cycle between 0 and 1, whence a negative self-loop on 3.

Acknowledgements. We thank Christophe Soulé and Denis Thieffry for helpful discussions.

References

1. Aracena, J.: Modèles mathématiques discrets associés à des systèmes biologiques. Application aux réseaux de régulation génétiques. Thèse de doctorat, Université Joseph Fourier, Grenoble (2001)
2. Chaouiya, C., Remy, É., Ruet, P., Thieffry, D.: Qualitative modelling of genetic networks: from logical regulatory graphs to standard Petri nets. In: Cortadella, J., Reisig, W. (eds.) ICATPN 2004. LNCS, vol. 3099, pp. 137–156. Springer, Heidelberg (2004)

3. Danos, V., Laneve, C.: Graphs for core molecular biology. In *Computational Methods in Systems Biology*. In: Priami, C. (ed.) CMSB 2003. LNCS, vol. 2602, pp. 34–46. Springer, Heidelberg (2003)

4. Gouzé, J.-L.: Positive and negative circuits in dynamical systems. Journal of Biological Systems 6, 11–15 (1998)

5. Karmakar, R., Bose, I.: Graded and binary responses in stochastic gene expression. Technical report, arXiv:q-bio. OT/0411012 (2004)

6. Li, F., Long, T., Lu, Y., Ouyang, Q., Tang, C.: The yeast cell-cycle network is robustly designed. In: Proceedings of the National Academy of Sciences of the United States of America (2004)

7. Markevich, N.I., Hoek, J.B., Kholodenko, B.N.: Signaling switches and bistability arising from multisite phosphorylation in protein kinase cascades. Journal of Cell Biology (2004)

8. Plahte, E., Mestl, T., Omholt, S.W.: Feedback loops, stability and multistationarity in dynamical systems. Journal Biological Systems 3, 409–413 (1995)

9. Remy, É., Ruet, P., Mendoza, L., Thieffry, D., Chaouiya, C.: From logical regulatory graphs to standard Petri nets: dynamical roles and functionality of feedback circuits. In: Priami, C., Ingólfsdóttir, A., Mishra, B., Nielson, H.R. (eds.) Transactions on Computational Systems Biology VII. LNCS (LNBI), vol. 4230, pp. 56–72. Springer, Heidelberg (2006)

10. Remy, É., Ruet, P., Thieffry, D.: Graphic requirements for multistability and attractive cycles in a Boolean dynamical framework. Under review, Prépublication Institut de Mathématiques de Luminy 2005-08 (2005), Available at http://iml.univ-mrs.fr/~ruet/papiers.html

11. Robert, F.: *Discrete iterations: a metric study*. Series in Computational Mathematics, vol. 6. Springer, Heidelberg (1986)

12. Robert, F.: Les systèmes dynamiques discrets. In: Robinet, B. (ed.) Programming Symposium. LNCS, vol. 19, Springer, Heidelberg (1974)

13. Shih, M.-H., Dong, J.-L.: A combinatorial analogue of the Jacobian problem in automata networks. Advances in Applied Mathematics 34(1), 30–46 (2005)

14. Snoussi, E.H.: Necessary conditions for multistationarity and stable periodicity. Journal of Biological Systems 6, 3–9 (1998)

15. Soulé, C.: Graphic requirements for multistationarity. ComPlexUs 1, 123–133 (2003)

16. Soulé, C.: Mathematical approaches to gene regulation and differentiation. (Manuscript 2005)

17. Thomas, R.: On the relation between the logical structure of systems and their ability to generate multiple steady states and sustained oscillations. In: Series in Synergetics, vol. 9, pp. 180–193. Springer, Heidelberg (1981)

Author Index

Lecture Notes in Bioinformatics